T0144615

DRIVEN
to
SUCCESS

A 10-Point Checkup for Achieving
High Performance in Business

Advance Praise for *Driven to Success*

"A no-nonsense, how-to, nuts-and-bolts guide for ensuring organizational alignment and high performance. Written in layman's terms so that business executives and frontline supervisors alike can understand and take immediate action. *Driven to Success* should be an essential part of every leader's toolkit."

Lori Addicks, Vice President
Learning and Development
Post Properties, Inc.

"A great operator's guide that lays out an excellent roadmap for leading a high-performance organization. The book brings all the important concepts together in a logical, easy-to–understand, and useable format. It makes perfect sense to use this book as a personal leadership book, and it is a terrific teaching tool for leadership training programs."

Major General William T. Nesbitt
The Adjutant General
Georgia Department of Defense

"There is more to being a visionary leader than what you can find in a book—however, this book is a great place to start. The 10-Point checkup is filled with practical thoughts and tools to focus the traveler."

Alan Kaye
Senior Vice President
Mattel, Inc.

"I recommend *Driven to Success* as a sound practical approach to achieving better performance regardless of the size of your department, business unit, or organization. In this book Dr. Goldner shows you how to uncover the organizational gaps and leadership assumptions that can be obstacles to achieving high performance. It is an accurate reflection of her consulting work over the past twenty-five years. I know firsthand."

Brian Wilkinson, Manager
Organizational Development
Cracker Barrel Old Country Store

"I was enlightened by Jane Goldner's easy-to-read, logical book. I loved the automobile metaphor throughout, which should resonate with anyone leading a business or with middle managers who lead teams and departments. In my business we deal with intangible products—songs. Dr. Goldner's information is very pertinent for what we do at BMI. It will remain a readily available reference guide for me."

Charlie Feldman, Vice President
Writer-Publisher Relations
BMI, New York

"People talk about the complexity of leadership … and that's because leadership is *people*. Learning to lead effectively is a lifelong challenge, and Dr. Goldner's book is a solid, powerful approach to meeting that objective. *Driven to Success* is a practical, tactical blueprint that can be used effectively in any organization."

Rebecca Clements, Vice President
Global Pricing Strategy and Business
Profitability
Elavon

DRIVEN
to
SUCCESS

A 10-Point Checkup for Achieving High Performance in Business

Jane S. Goldner, PhD

New York

Driven to Success

A 10-Point Checkup for Achieving High Performance in Buiness

Copyright 2009 Jane S. Goldner, PhD. All rights reserved.

No part of this publication may be reproduced or transmitted in any form or by any means, mechanical or electronic, including photocopying and recording, or by any information storage and retrieval system, without permission in writing from the author or publisher (except by a reviewer, who may quote brief passages and/or short brief video clips in a review.)

Disclaimer: The Publisher and the Author make no representations or warranties with respect to the accuracy or completeness of the contents of this work and specifically disclaim all warranties, including without limitation warranties of fitness for a particular purpose. No warranty may be created or extended by sales or promotional materials. The advice and strategies contained herein may not be suitable for every situation. This work is sold with the understanding that the Publisher is not engaged in rendering legal, accounting, or other professional services. If professional assistance is required, the services of a competent professional person should be sought. Neither the Publisher nor the Author shall be liable for damages arising herefrom. The fact that an organization or website is referred to in this work as a citation and/or a potential source of further information does not mean that the Author or the Publisher endorses the information the organization or website may provide or recommendations it may make. Further, readers should be aware that internet websites listed in this work may have changed or disappeared between when this work was written and when it is read.

Library of Congress Control Number: 2008941915

ISBN 978-1-60037-550-7

The Business Operating System Solution for
Enterprise Results (BOSS©) copyright of Jane S. Goldner, PhD

MORGAN · JAMES
THE ENTREPRENEURIAL PUBLISHER

Morgan James Publishing, LLC
1225 Franklin Ave., STE 325
Garden City, NY 11530-1693
Toll Free 800-485-4943
www.MorganJamesPublishing.com

In an effort to support local communities, raise awareness and funds, Morgan James Publishing donates one percent of all book sales for the life of each book to Habitat for Humanity. Get involved today, visit **www.HelpHabitatForHumanity.org**.

Dedication

This book is dedicated to the three men in my life: my husband Steve and my two sons Andy and Greg, who have heard about this book for so long that they can't believe it's finally in print. I couldn't have done it without their love, support, and an occasional "kick in the pants."

Contents

Foreword

It doesn't matter if you're talking about auto racing, professional sports, or business; the differential between high performers and those who get left behind is very small. The difference between those who win and those who also ran comes down to executing well on a few fundamentals.

Having been part of a fast growing family-owned business, the turnaround of a medium-sized business, and the transformation of the division of a Fortune 100 company struggling with its monopolistic past, I learned through trial and error what drives results and sustains high performance. Though I was successful in all, it would have been very helpful to have had this book on my shelf. *Driven to Success* provides a step-by-step guide for ensuring business success. It starts with an assessment of your current effectiveness and then leads you through a practical process to make sure your engine is firing on all cylinders. Dr. Goldner lays out important fundamentals in an easy-to-read format of ten key checkpoints.

After more than thirty years in business, I, too, am convinced that success comes down to just a few things, beginning with Dr. Goldner's Checkpoint 2, communicating the core. Don't ask a team to run a race and not tell them where the stadium is (mission); make sure they know where the finish line is (vision) and what the rules are for getting there (values). These terms may be overused today, but for business excellence, their essence cannot be overcommunicated. So, if you're ready to rev up your business, fine-tune your engine, and supercharge your performance, read on. What separates those who win and those who don't is often measured in a photo finish, but if you read *Driven to Success* and follow its timeless advice, the checkered flag will be waving for you.

Fred Shaftman, President
BellSouth, Large Business Services
Corporate Officer, Retired

Preface

CONGRATULATIONS! You have an opportunity to drive your business to the next level of performance. It is one of the best investments that you'll make for your company. To start your journey, read this book. In it you will learn how to create (ready), connect (set), and communicate (go) the infrastructure that will enable your business to achieve high performance.

Keep this book nearby so you can refer to it at any time. Maintaining the high performance of your company requires periodic maintenance checkups. We have included a "parts inventory" for that purpose. Use it on an ongoing basis to preserve your investment and drive high performance trouble free.

Driven to Success covers all models (types and sizes of businesses). The words *business, company*, and *organization* are used interchangeably throughout the book. You may find that you need to modify some of the features to fit your company's specific needs. If some of the words are not familiar to you, check the glossary at the back of the book. This information and the specifications have been developed over twenty-five years working with all makes and models of organizations. It is the best of what we know and do.

We are dedicated to your satisfaction. If at any time you need assistance, The Goldner Group has staff specifically trained in the processes of the Business Operating System Solution (BOSS). We are pleased to answer any questions or come on site to assist you. You can reach us at (404) 459-2860 or info@thegoldnergroup.com.

The Goldner Group

Acknowledgments

No one writes and publishes a book alone. My heartfelt thanks go to Lori Addicks, Post Properties, Inc.; Jodie Charlop, potentialmatters; Chris Gilliam, The Gilliam Group; Alan Kaye, Mattel, Inc.; Major General William T. Nesbitt, The Georgia Department of Defense; Morene Seldes-Marcus, MSM Consulting; and Brian Wilkinson, Cracker Barrel Old Country Store. Their feedback was both inspirational and instructive. In addition, recognition goes to Willy Spizman, the Spizman Agency, and to the team at Morgan James Publishing who made the final product possible.

Introduction

Who Should Read This Book?

☐ *Owners of mom-and-pop companies that can't run by osmosis any more.* You've started a business, figured out your market niche, and hired employees. Going to the next level requires assessing what you must do differently to be successful as you grow. Otherwise you'll stay self-employed.

☐ *Owners of small companies growing to their next stage of business.* You've grown your business. Now you need to continue to build the infrastructure of your company by putting systems in place to take your business to the next level and make it sustainable.

☐ *Leaders of midsize companies growing to the next level of business.* Resting on your past success will get you run over by others who know that continuously upgrading infrastructure systems is a critical key to sustained success.

☐ *Leaders of divisions of larger companies who want to grow the business.* To be truly successful in making the necessary changes, you have to have the authority to affect the infrastructure of your division.

☐ *Visionary leaders who are getting results but know that they can do better.* Going to the next level requires investing in becoming more systematic through your company's infrastructure. It takes commitment, introspection, and a thoughtful approach. *Driven to Success* will show you how.

Small Is the New Big

There are many books on high performance written for large organizations. Much can be learned from them around the need for structure. However, small is the new big. Small companies can be fluid across company boundaries, fast to the market, and flexible in meeting customer expectations. These advantageous attributes for success come more naturally to smaller companies. The internal structure comes with more difficulty. *Driven to Success* focuses on helping you maintain the advantage by creating the winning balance between small-company attributes and large-company internal structure.

The Model at a Glance

The Business Operating System Solution for Enterprise Results (BOSS)

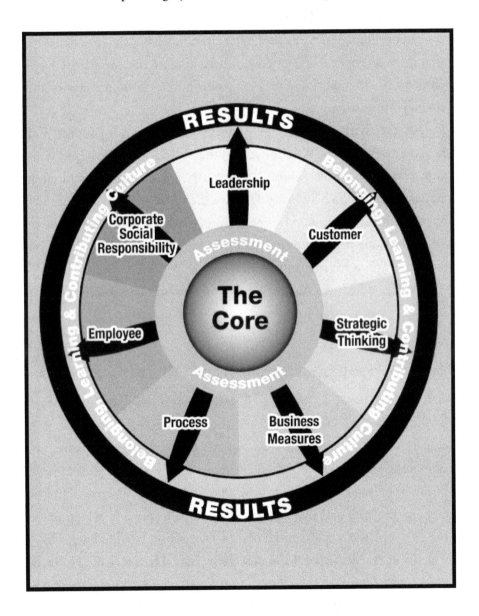

BOSS Model Highlights

Most people select a high-performance car for looks and engineering. They would not make the investment without knowing what's under the hood. Just as with a high-performance car, there are two parts of company success: the business of the company (products and services, the exterior look of the business to its customers) and the infrastructure (the internal systems, the interior functioning of the company). Both parts together support business success. The BOSS model creates the enabling infrastructure.

All the systems of a high-performance car must connect and function well. The BOSS connects all the individual initiatives in your company. This book guides you through creating well-functioning systems. The BOSS Model breaks down silos/stovepipes by functioning as the communication and information vehicle. It allows everyone to be on the same page, communicating and interacting using a common language. It is a relationship facilitator.

The BOSS Model turns the power of one into the power of many. It gives you the extra horsepower you need to win the race.

Twenty-First-Century Models and Driving Conditions

A few years ago, GM introduced a commercial that declared, "This isn't your father's Oldsmobile." As true as that was then for cars, it is equally true for companies now. Twenty-first-century companies are significantly different from their predecessors. This *is not* your father's business. At the beginning of the 1990s, Jack Welch, Jr., past CEO of General Electric, said that the pace of change in the '90s would make the '80s look like a walk in the park. Competition would be relentless. The bar of excellence would be raised every day. He was right. The early twenty-first century is telling us to forget walking or running; we're not even in the park. We have been ratcheting and continue to ratchet up the chaos of organization life. We operate in a world of uncertainty and accelerating change. Just look around you; read the newspapers; turn on the television. Competition is fierce; markets are merciless. Economics are based on intellectual capital. Earlier we said that small is the new big. Small companies outsmart large corporations on a global scale. Customers have infinite access to products, services, and information. They continue to demand faster, cheaper, and better products and services. You will need to do business in real time or *you will die*. So, what's a leader to do?

In *Rethinking the Future*, Rowen Gibson described a very different successful company. It is smaller and networked with decentralized profit centers. The culture is one of high trust and has a learning infrastructure. People are utilized wherever they're needed, and are treated like owners. The challenge is to combine the discipline necessary to run the business with the freedom that allows individuals to excel. The answer lies in the need to create a company landscape that is uniquely your own. "Me, too" companies will no longer be winners. To paraphrase author Charles Handy, the winners will be those who invent the world, not respond to it.

These driving conditions equate to a great deal of off-road driving, often without a roadmap. So buckle up and get ready to take off.

What Does It Take to Be in the Driver's Seat?

High-performance leaders need to have passion and a vision. They should be looking forward, scanning the landscape, watching the competition, and quickly but thoughtfully taking advantage of new opportunities while setting trends, acting nothing like a me, too company. Leaders need to leverage technology for interaction and real-time connection with the marketplace, get and use feedback, and use intuition as much as analysis to react to information. Most of all, leaders need to embrace and create proactive, continuous change and a collaborative culture. They should be comfortable with discontinuity and use it to create trend-setting opportunities. Again, the question is so what's a leader to do in face of the breakneck speed, nothing-like-your-father's-business scenario? *Become a new powerful leader*, one whose leadership is very different from your father's powerful leadership. Get out of your father's car and into your own twenty-first-century high-performance vehicle.

Detailed Driver Information

Powerful leadership has been redefined. Drivers of high performance create healthy, cohesive, and successful companies that leave a lasting legacy. Their secret lies in the ability to develop a culture in which people want to belong, learn, and contribute. That starts with the leaders' thoughtful reflection about the future and their leadership approach. It is no longer about power over others. It is about the fact that the more power you give away, the more powerful you become and the more powerful results your business can produce. Powerful leadership includes harnessing and releasing the capabilities of people by pushing information, responsibility, authority, trust, and recognition throughout the company. It means creating power for you as well as helping others gain power in order to contribute to the business. That takes a thoughtful approach. From thoughtful reflection comes effective action; that is different from "ready, fire, aim."

Powerful leaders believe the following:

☐ They must be the primary role models.

☐ Everyone needs to be passionate and focused on the core (mission, vision, values).

☐ All initiatives need to be integrated.

☐ They must continually assess where the business is as compared to the core

☐ Continuous sharing of information throughout the company is critical.

- ☐ Everyone in the company needs to embrace ongoing change.
- ☐ They must create a culture of belonging, learning, and contributing.
- ☐ They create and leave a positive legacy in their companies.

It seems so basic. So why aren't more leaders truly powerful? *You* are a leader. Ask yourself, why am I not taking time for thoughtful reflection or taking aim before firing? Over the years, we have heard three common reasons:

1. I'm doing what my past bosses have done.
2. I have no time to do leadership.
3. I've delegated that responsibility.

The days of successful autocratic leadership where leaders think and employees do are gone. Consumers want better, more cost-effective products faster. You can no longer do it yourself. No wonder so many talented people are leaving organizations to start their own companies or to join start-ups to feel a sense of ownership. Leadership is your job. You are no longer a technician or an individual contributor. Your leadership is woven into the fabric of how you do business to be successful. It is not an extra responsibility if you have time. There are certain responsibilities that cannot be delegated, and leadership is one of them. Having a vision of the right tomorrow and mobilizing and empowering people are *your* job. To be a truly powerful leader, you must be able to answer the following questions affirmatively:

- ☐ Do I have a clear vision of a successful future for the business? Am I passionate about it?
- ☐ Have I defined a legacy that I want to leave for my company?
- ☐ Do I recognize my own strengths and liabilities? How do I know my perceptions are accurate?

- ☐ Have I continued my own learning?

- ☐ Have I surrounded myself with the right leadership team?

- ☐ Can we clearly articulate who our customers are and what they need, want, and expect?

- ☐ Do we have a plan to work our mission and achieve our vision?

- ☐ Are we able to determine the levels of our success on an ongoing basis? Do we celebrate successes along the way?

- ☐ Do we have an integrated approach to leading our company?

- ☐ Do we have the right company structure in place that allows people to do their best work?

- ☐ Have we taken action to contribute to the sustainability of the earth's resources as well as to contribute to the surrounding community in which we operate?

- ☐ Have we created a culture in which people want to belong, learn, and contribute?

If you answered yes to any of these questions, how do you know it's true? What are your metrics?

The success of powerful leadership rests on the foundation of shared commitment to the mission, vision, and values that define the right tomorrow. The ability of your company to reach its vision depends upon your capacity to recognize your own limitations and appreciate the strengths of others. You must ante up first because it all starts with you. It takes your willingness to step away from the quick, easy fix and move toward a reflective, thoughtful approach. Are you willing to take the necessary steps to become a powerful leader? If so, read on.

This book is about being the leader that others want to follow, one for whom they want to go the extra mile. Have you ever wondered why some companies seem to win the races and thrive amidst the trials and tribulations of the twenty-first-century business life while others thrash about in pain and frustration going from crisis to crisis? If so, *Driven to Success* will help you guide your company to becoming one that thrives.

Will you be one of those powerful leaders who creates a healthy, cohesive, and successful company? That depends partly on how willing you are to look under the hood of your business and implement the actions in each part of the 10-point checkup and partly on how committed you are to holding the people in your company accountable for doing the same.

Safety Tips for Leaders

Be an authentic leader. The information in this book is not about suggesting that you change who you are. It is about guiding you on the journey of using your own personality to create a successful business that drives high-performance results.

Don't start what you don't intend to finish. It's better to do it right the first time than to do it over. Doing it over translates into lost credibility with your stakeholders and a poor return on investment. You have finite resources. Use them wisely.

Build on what is already working. You have built a successful business. Identify and keep what you are doing that is already working well, but don't hesitate to shake things up.

The foundation for success is like the four tires on a high-performance car. If a tire is low on air, it will slow you down. If you lose a tire, you'll veer off course. Either way, you'll end up in crisis. The four tires of leadership success are

1. Trust in leaders
2. Belief that things will be great
3. Two-way communication for information and feedback
4. Pride in accomplishments

Pay attention to the three Cs of successful initiatives. Create the initiative tailored to your company instead of adopting an off-the-shelf solution. Connect all initiatives to one another and, most important, to the core. Communicate so that people in your company can act on the initiatives. (You will see these three Cs repeated in the form of "high-performance actions" at the end of each checkpoint.)

Consultants can add value when they come to visit but don't live with you. Use consultants at critical trigger points. Their deliverable should be to build capacity in your company rather than make you dependent on them.

So ... drive on.

Legend

At each **checkpoint** you will see

- ☐ The model (**The Business Operating System Solution for Enterprise Results/BOSS**) with the relevant **checkpoint** highlighted

- ☐ The pieces of the **BOSS Parts Inventory** that relate to the **checkpoint**

- ☐ **Important Information** to know about the **checkpoint**

- ☐ A **Passing Lane** for those who don't choose to read the narrative information but just want the key points

- ☐ **Off-Road Successes** that are examples of **BOSS** practices

- ☐ **High-Performance Actions** that are the three Cs (*create, connect, communicate*) for you to act on if you want to take your business to the next level, where the rubber meets the road

- ☐ A **Driving Tip** that is a practical application of the **checkpoint**

DRIVEN
to
SUCCESS

CHECKPOINT 1:

Assessing How Well Your Company Is Doing

Important Information

Oil changes, 7,500-mile checkup, 15,000-mile checkup, 30,000-mile checkup—you get the picture. Periodically, you have to stop and take your car in to a professional for a maintenance checkup to assure the best driving performance. Your company is no different.

Creating a high-performance company begins with a thorough checkup of the infrastructure. Objective assessment provides the answer to the questions, how well is your company doing? and how do you know? A leader in a technology company once told me, "There is an inherent flaw in companies observing and critiquing themselves. Those responsible for the problem/issue are not likely to see it and/or are not willing to admit that there is a problem." All too often leaders think that they know how their businesses are doing, but what they typically have are partial answers.

Partial answers can get you into trouble. The higher up you sit in the company, the more filtered your information becomes. We've learned that lesson from interviewing individual contributors and first-line supervisors who are closest to the customers. A common and interesting response has been, senior leaders filter what they tell the head of the company. Most of the time, it's only the good news. Now, that causes me to ask, why? Is there a history of shooting the messenger? (Do you shoot the messenger?) I once worked with the president of a company who told me that every time I came into his office he put a bottle of Advil on his desk. My response was twofold. One, he hired me to tell him the truth. Two, if he wanted agreement, he had plenty of yes people surrounding him. This story speaks to the point of objective assessment if you want high-performance results. If moderate to good is okay, then partial truths will suffice.

You're now asking, assess what? Appropriate question. The answer? Evaluate the key performance areas of the infrastructure in your company. The core, for example, is the changeless North Star, which tells you if you are heading in the right direction. It's the one constant on which you can rely in a world that is forcing relentless, fast-paced change. The core allows you to constantly modify strategies and actions as external and internal conditions change. It is what all other pieces are assessed against. (More about the core in the next checkpoint.) Connecting all the pieces of the infrastructure to the core is critical. Too many companies try to evaluate and improve the components without looking at the impact of the whole system. They tackle each piece as a project without determining the interrelationships.

You know what to change or improve through continuous objective assessment. While objective assessment provides complete answers, a leader can start with an internal assessment to get the lay of the land.

Passing Lane

☐ Like a high-performance car, your business requires periodic maintenance checkups.

☐ While self-assessment is a way to start your journey, objective assessment by a third party results in data that is more honest.

☐ Ensure that each initiative is connected to the core of your company and to each other, as appropriate.

☐ Start at the appropriate place to improve your company. Set realistic priorities and goals to get to the next level.

High-Performance Actions

Ready: Create

- ☐ Complete a scheduled checkup using The BOSS Parts Inventory (pages 26-29) as a starting point. Ask members of your leadership team to do the same.

- ☐ Compare results. Are you all on the same page?

- ☐ What do you currently have in place?

- ☐ Reflect on how satisfied you are with its usefulness.

Set: Connect

- ☐ Is each initiative connected to the core of your company?

- ☐ Is each one focused on helping you work your mission and achieve your vision?

- ☐ Does each one reflect the values?

Go: Communicate

- ☐ Meet with your leadership team to discuss the results and determine which areas need attention because either nothing is being done or you are not satisfied with the results.

- ☐ You may want to also ask employees to complete the BOSS checkup. Depending on where you sit in the company, your view will be different.

Driving Tip

Be sure to include other people in your company in the assessment to gain a cross section of perspectives. Your company may look different at the top. Use the checklist as a starting point. Then hold focus groups to drill down on key issues.

Scheduled Maintenance Checkup

The Business Operating System Solution for Enterprise Results (BOSS)

Parts Inventory

Read the inventory items on the following pages and put a checkmark in the box beside each statement you believe to be in place in your company. Then revisit each item and ask yourself if you are satisfied with the results you are seeing.

In Place	Satisfied	Checkpoint
		The Core
☐	☐	We have communicated a mission so that everyone knows what business we are in.
☐	☐	We have communicated a vision so that everyone knows where we are heading.
☐	☐	We have communicated a set of values so that everyone in the company knows what's important and what is acceptable behavior.
		Leadership
☐	☐	The company has effective leaders in place.
☐	☐	Leadership roles, responsibilities, and core competencies are clearly defined (including my own) according to the mission, vision, and values.
☐	☐	Leaders consistently demonstrate the core competencies.
☐	☐	I have communicated the legacy that I want to leave to the company.
☐	☐	Leaders encourage individuals to be creative and innovative to meet customer expectations, including problem solving for customers.
☐	☐	Leaders provide for their own continuing development.

In Place	Satisfied	Checkpoint
☐	☐	Leaders provide and support the continuing development of employees.
☐	☐	We have a process in place for creating a pool of future leaders.

Customers

In Place	Satisfied	Checkpoint
☐	☐	Everyone knows who the company's customers are as well as their specific customers.
☐	☐	We understand customer and stakeholder expectations.
☐	☐	We have a system in place for ongoing communication with our customers and stakeholders.
☐	☐	We use the customer and stakeholder data to make changes/improvements.
☐	☐	Our customers and stakeholders view us as trustworthy and reliable.
☐	☐	Customers and stakeholders have a high level of loyalty to our products and services.

Strategic Thinking

In Place	Satisfied	Checkpoint
☐	☐	Everyone in the company is a strategic thinker. Everyone considers how decisions today affect tomorrow.
☐	☐	We have developed and continuously update a strategic framework according to our customers' expectations and our mission, vision, and values.
☐	☐	The strategic framework is shared throughout the company.
☐	☐	Leaders have articulated the strategic framework so that everyone understands how individual and team objectives contribute to the framework.

27

In Place	Satisfied	Checkpoint
		Measures
☐	☐	There is a system in place to track and review business performance and capabilities, based on our strategic framework, on an ongoing basis.
☐	☐	We track and review a dashboard of measures, not just financial measures.
☐	☐	We are satisfied with our business results.
		Processes
☐	☐	We have all the technology, facilities, and equipment that we need to excel.
☐	☐	Our processes are clearly defined.
☐	☐	Our processes are customer focused.
☐	☐	Our processes are defined so that our employees are able to do their best work.
☐	☐	The company has a process in place for continuous improvement and innovation based on customers' expectations.
		Employees
☐	☐	We have defined the skills, abilities, and culture-fit priorities our company needs for success based on our mission, vision, and values.
☐	☐	We hire according to these established needs.
☐	☐	We are able to attract and retain the people we need.
☐	☐	Each employee has individual and team-performance objectives that directly relate and contribute to the desired results defined in the strategic framework.

In Place	Satisfied	Checkpoint
☐	☐	People in the company are expected to be accountable for their objectives, performance, and results.
☐	☐	We have a system in place for ongoing two-way communication with our employees.
☐	☐	Company and job-relevant information is readily available to our employees.
☐	☐	There is a system in place for providing ongoing feedback to employees on performance.
☐	☐	People in the company are rewarded for their performance based on their objectives (individual, team, and company).

Corporate Social Responsibility

In Place	Satisfied	
☐	☐	We increase the size of our social and economic tire track by participating in activities that support the surrounding communities in which we operate.
☐	☐	Our company and its processes are designed to decrease the environmental tire track we leave on the earth's resources.

Corporate Culture

In Place	Satisfied	
☐	☐	Our leaders have created a culture in which employees want to belong.
☐	☐	Our leaders have created a culture in which employees want to continuously learn.
☐	☐	Our leaders have created a culture in which employees want to contribute to the success of the business.

Beginning with Checkpoint 2, the core, review your answers to the parts inventory at the beginning of each checkpoint before proceeding.

CHECKPOINT 2:

Defining and Articulating the Core of Your Company

Parts Inventory

☐ We have communicated a mission so that everyone knows what business we are in.

☐ We have communicated a vision so that everyone knows where we are heading.

☐ We have communicated a set of values so that everyone in the company knows what's important and what is acceptable behavior.

Important Information

The most significant piece of The BOSS is the core (mission, vision, and values) of your company. Like the chassis of a car, it is the foundation upon which the other parts rest. The core provides a clear, common focus and direction. If everyone in your company understood it and found his or her place within it, you wouldn't need micromanaging or volumes of policies and procedures manuals to tell people what to do and how to act. In fact, if all your stakeholders knew it, they would be clear on your company's added value to them. Recently we completed an intensive customer survey for a client. One key finding was that many of its customers were not at all aware of the range of services provided by the organization or why customers should call them instead of their competition. Confirming and communicating the core was the first step in responding to the lack of clarity.

A cartoon circulating depicts Moses standing on top of a mountain holding the Ten Commandments. The people at the foot of the mountain are looking up saying, *"Oh, no, not another vision statement!"* Oftentimes people in companies think exactly like that. Their senior leaders have gone off to some retreat and come back with the latest and greatest mission, vision, and set of values. Fairly soon, like their predecessors, these declarations collect dust on the leaders' bookshelves or on the walls of the company. At best, they hang on the walls to cover the holes from the previous edits. Witness Enron, WorldCom, and Adelphia, among others. I'm fairly certain that they all had mission, vision, and value statements hung on the walls. But something was missing that caused these companies to tumble. The missing link was the connection between words and action. This disconnect starts at the very beginning of the process of developing the core when leaders do not take into account the need to

- Ante up the behaviors first
- Communicate the mission, vision, and values in a way that connects each person to it
- Explain how their jobs contribute to the core of the business
- Obtain buy in and support

Remember, the mission defines the purpose of the business. The vision determines what it could be at its best if everyone were firing on all cylinders. The values not only define acceptable behavior inside and outside of the company but also determines the rightness or wrongness of the direction the leaders have chosen. Wouldn't this information have been helpful to the leaders of Enron, WorldCom, and Adelphia, especially if they walked their talk?

When asked to define a compelling future for their businesses, many leaders get a deer-in-the-headlights look. Do you? Is it the word *compelling*? Or is it the absence of a vision of the future? If you cannot articulate the desired direction for your organization, who can? Perhaps you can't define it because you haven't taken time to define your own core.

Effective leadership is about knowing who you are, what is important to you, where you want to go and then aligning that with the core of your company. The result of that alignment is called passion. You spend too much time at work not to be passionate about where you go and what you do every day. Leaders need passion to steer their companies to higher performance.

How do you discover your own core, your personal mission, vision, and values? *Reflection.* Too many leaders go from crisis to crisis, never stopping to think back on the events. What went right? What went wrong? How could we do things differently next time? What are the lessons learned? The army calls this process an after-action review . Those who don't go through this reflective process and learn from it are doomed to repeat the same or similar mistakes.

The same holds true for reflection about oneself. Too many leaders don't take the time to define their own cores much less connect them to the core of their companies. What's missing for them is passion. If it's missing in the leader, it's missing in the rest of the people in the organization. That's no way to get better and better results. How do you create your own mission, vision, and values statements? Take some time for thoughtful reflection and answer the following questions:

- What is your purpose? What do you want to be remembered for in your work life and in life in general?

- What do you imagine your own future will be? What could you be at your best if you were living out your purpose and acting on your values?

- What are your values? What is important to you? What are those few gut behaviors that you wouldn't trade even if you were in a back-against-the-wall situation?

Now, examine the core of your company. Haven't defined it yet or not satisfied with what exists? (Check your BOSS Scheduled Maintenance Checkup that you previously completed.) It's the leader's responsibility to define the core after input from people in the company. Input up front is important for buy in and support later on. Here are the steps to creating a meaningful mission, vision, and set of values.

1. Bring the appropriate people together. (Sometimes, it's just senior leadership; other times, informal leaders from throughout the company are included.)

2. Define or review the mission of your business and why it exists. Said another way, what wouldn't get done if your company didn't exist? Include your company's products and services, your target customers and the key value added to those customers. You will be amazed at how quickly your mission statement can be developed. Don't spend a great deal of time trying to wordsmith while creating the draft (that's what subteams are for).

3. Next, answer the question, "If we were working at our optimum level, firing on all cylinders, what could our company be?" A vision is the clear picture of the "end state" of where you want to take the company. Think of the vision as a painting, one that when each person looks at it, the interpretation is clear. Again, beware of trying to be wordsmiths like one of our clients who spent half a day arguing

about whether or not to include the phrase "world class" in their vision statement. Keep it short enough to be memorable so everyone in your company can remember it as they go through their day-to-day decision making. If you must have a long explanation of your vision (like another one of our clients who had a two page story of his company in the year 2010), be willing to condense it to a "hang tag" that people can remember. The bottom line is that the vision has to be meaningful to individuals within your company, something to strive for that is challenging and creates passion.

4. Define the collective beliefs about how people in your company, especially the leaders, think the world works. Beliefs drive values. For example, do you believe that people come to work just for a paycheck and need to be micromanaged in order to do a good job or do you believe they come to work wanting to do a good job and will if given the appropriate responsibility, authority and resources? Is it okay that some people

   ☐ Work to live?

   ☐ Live to work?

   ☐ Do a combination?

Do you believe that your company is part of a larger community system or do you believe that your company is an entity apart from the community in which it operates?

Once you've fleshed out all the beliefs with your designated team (which is an interesting exercise in itself to determine if everyone is on the same page), then it's time to determine the values that are important to your company's success. Values are those behavioral guidelines that determine how people are expected to work and play together. Equally as important, they dictate appropriate behavior with your customers. Again, think of Enron versus Johnson & Johnson during the Tylenol problem. In which organization would you rather work and be proud of having a leadership role? The whistleblower in Enron was being interviewed on a talk show soon after the debacle. The interviewer asked this individual, "What advice would you give your daughter as she enters the world of work?" Without hesitation, she responded that she would advise her to find out about the values of the company during the interview process. And if they didn't match hers, to run away as fast as she could. Do you want people running toward or away from your company?

Now that you have defined your own core and that of your organization, think about the similarities between the two. What is the connection between your core and the core of the company? Can you bring and live out your core every day at work? What excites you about being a leader in your company?

Your job now is only half done. What remains is communicating the mission, vision, and values to the rest of the people in your company, giving them an opportunity to align their own cores with that of the business. In fact, one of your key responsibilities is to be on a constant soapbox about the core, ensuring that each person is making day-to-day decisions that propel the company toward its vision.

Remember, while mission, vision, and values are leader initiated, each person needs to find her or his place in them. Once connected, each person can support the core of the company. A compelling shared core is essential for high-performance results. Lastly, remember that everything you do, all the initiatives in the company, should be evaluated against the core. If an initiative doesn't reinforce the mission, move the business toward its vision; if it is not aligned with the values, ask yourself, why are we doing this? Why are we spending our resources, time, and money on it?

Passing Lane

- ☐ The core is the chassis, the foundation upon which all the other parts rest.

- ☐ The core provides a clear, common focus and direction for your company. It is true north on your compass against which everything else is assessed.

- ☐ The core consists of the mission, vision, and values.

- ☐ The mission defines what business you are in, the purpose of your company, why it exists.

- ☐ The vision describes what your company could be at its best if everyone were firing on all cylinders.

- ☐ Values drive behavior about how you want everyone in your company, including yourself, to treat customers and each other. Values also determine the rightness or wrongness of the direction you are taking your company.

- ☐ It is important for you, as the key leader of your company, to know your own core and how it aligns with the core of your company.

- ☐ All these points won't get you a return on your efforts until the core of the company is communicated and each employee has the opportunity to align her or his core with that of the company's.

Off-Road Successes

- ☐ An environmental testing business began as a three-person operation. The strategy was to accept all business, to never say no. The goal was to keep the doors open and grow a viable company. As it grew to over a $10-million business, the old strategy became debilitating. The company had many small clients, but the business was all over the place, without focus. The first step was to define the core. The mission and vision clarified the business the leadership wanted to build and defined how they wanted to position themselves for the future. This clarity focused their decisions on yes and no, what businesses to keep and what to divest. These decisions helped them to grow to over a $30-million business with more than three hundred employees within a short period.

- ☐ Another example of core practices is an engineering firm that presents a PVV (purpose, values, and vision) award to associates who exhibit the company's core values in their work. Four individuals and four project teams can earn this award at any given time. The coveted award includes both money and a trophy.

High-Performance Actions

Ready: Create

- ☐ Define *your* core.

- ☐ Create the company core using the appropriate process and people.

Set: Connect

- ☐ Examine your core against the company core.

- ☐ Ensure that every business strategy, activity, and resource is connected to the company core.

Go: Communicate

- ☐ Hold meetings with employees to communicate the company mission, vision, and values.

- ☐ Use multiple ways to remind employees of the company core. Place it on the homepage of your company intranet, on coffee mugs and paperweights.

- ☐ Allow people time to define their own cores and relate to the company core.

- ☐ Be on a soapbox about the core.

Driving Tip

One of our clients includes the core question at every leadership meeting. He asks each person around the table, what did you do this week that moved us closer to our vision? It elevates the conversation to a higher level than this week's crisis and reinforces the notion that defining the core is not a one-time event. It is a living, breathing representation of what the company is all about.

Driving Tip

After you create the mission statement, send it out to the other people in your company with the words "CHALLENGE IT" in bold caps at the top of the page. Give others the opportunity to react to the draft. It creates buy in. Do the same with the vision statement. Everyone needs to be passionate about these critical pieces, so give others a chance to react. The intent and direction of the business won't change. Usually, it's the passion around the words.

CHECKPOINT 3:

Developing the Current and Next Generation of Leaders

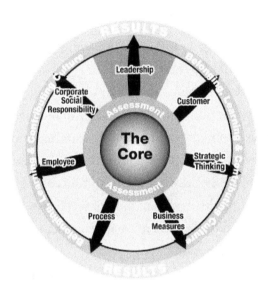

Parts Inventory

- ☐ The company has effective leaders in place.

- ☐ Leadership roles, responsibilities, and core competencies are clearly defined (including my own) according to the mission, vision, and values.

- ☐ Leaders consistently demonstrate the core competencies.

- ☐ I have communicated the legacy that I want to leave to the company.

- ☐ Leaders encourage individuals to be creative and innovative in helping to meet customer expectations, including problem solving for customers.

□ Leaders provide for their own continuing development of employees.

□ We have a process in place for creating a pool of future leaders.

Important Information

Effective leadership creates effective companies. Leaders are the steering wheel of the business, maintaining focus and direction. The most important responsibility of a leader like you is to ensure the long-term viability of your business. A key strategy to successfully execute this charge is the development of current and future leaders. Leaders are the reflection in the mirror of their companies. They determine whether the company will be healthy, cohesive, and successful by their actions. There is no avoiding the truth that, do as I say, not as I do doesn't work anymore (if it ever did). Leaders must ante up first in modeling the way and showing others the path.

Leadership development begins with determining what legacy you want to leave in your company. You don't have a choice as to whether you will leave a legacy because everyone does. You can, however, choose whether you will leave a positive or negative one. Your legacy is not so much determined by how long you have been with a company but the impact you make on others while you are there. A good starting point for figuring out what legacy you want to leave is your individual core. It is the bottom line of who you are and what you bring to any situation, including the leadership of your company. Revisit your core often, first to define your legacy and then to ensure that you are continually on track.

Once your legacy is defined, assess what strengths and blind spots you bring to the business. We have found the Myers-Briggs Type Indicator(www.mbti.com) to be a helpful instrument in this assessment, but many others will serve the same purpose. Next, answer what you are doing to continue your own learning. Development plans aren't just for everyone else in the company. What are *your* plans? Remember, ante up first and *then* blaze the trail.

After you have a clear understanding of what you do and don't bring to the table (we all like to think that we bring it all, but we don't), the next question is who have you surrounded yourself with on your leadership team? This action sends clear messages to the rest of the company. Many leaders hire in their own image, and why not? We like us, so we like people who are like us. However, this approach is the formula for disaster. First, if we hire in our own image, then we are bringing people onto our teams who have the same strengths and the same weaknesses. This leaves the team with gaping blind spots and, potentially, poor decision making. For example, many of our clients do not have a person on their team who will ask the question, how will the people in the company react to this decision? The team may wonder why it encounters resistance and many times failure of potentially significant initiatives. It doesn't mean that you don't do the initiative. It requires that you develop a strategy to deal with potential resistance.

A second message sent to people in the company when we hire in our own image is that diversity is not valued. Diversity includes not only ethnicity, gender, and age (the typical categories that we think about) but also personality types, ideas, and religion, to name several more categories. One client, who is president of his own company, holds Bible study at each leadership team meeting. Some people in his company have confided in me that they could never be on that team because they have different beliefs and would feel uncomfortable at meetings. Think of the potential talent this president is losing because of his lack of awareness or appreciation for the value of diversity.

Once you define your legacy, complete an assessment of your own strengths and weaknesses, and have an understanding of the makeup of your leadership team, you are ready to create a dynamic leadership development process—one that is systematic and repeatable and will ensure bench strength now and in the future.

What most leaders miss is that leadership development for others begins the first day a potential employee walks through the doors. It starts in the interviewing and hiring process. More potential leaders leave a company not because of a lack of skills to do the job but because of a poor cultural fit. Had the interviewer asked the appropriate questions, the mismatch may have been discovered during the initial process rather than after time and money had been spent orienting and taking the employee through the learning curve.

Skills are transportable from one company to the next; culture is not. For example, the vision of one of our clients requires that everyone step up to a role of leadership, including individual contributors. The organization is not only being hit with increasing customer demands and decreasing revenues but also facing the imminent retirement of several hundred leaders who are baby boomers. (More about baby boomers in Checkpoint 8.) It is imperative that they bring people on board who are able to meet the challenge of stepping up to leadership and who are capable of becoming formal leaders with increasing responsibilities in the near future. This mandate requires interview questions related to each candidate's leadership experience and abilities.

The best interview questions relate to real experience, not hypothetical situations. Interviewees are often very schooled in how to respond to questions, so make-believe questions are easy to answer. The real information comes from questions such as, tell me a time when you … . Press for specifics if the answer is vague. For the client previously mentioned, a good question would be, tell me a time when you were not in a formal position of leadership and you had to assume a leadership role. Describe the circumstances, what you did, and the outcome. You can also ask candidates about a time when their experiences did not go well and how they recovered if, in fact, they were able to turn the situation around. There are many available resources on behavioral-based interviewing. (See Further Reading.)

Another example from a client's experience is the hiring of a human resource director. The company had finally grown to the size that it needed a full-time person and hired an individual from a Fortune 100 company who was accustomed to large budgets and staffs. She was coming into a situation where she was the only HR person with a very small budget. The turnover was predictable because of the poor culture fit.

Once hired into the company, all leaders must first be a leader of self, as we have previously discussed. They need to be clear about their own cores and how they fit into the core of the company. Leaders must be aware of their own strengths and liabilities and have an ongoing development plan to leverage those strengths and compensate for liabilities. There are probably as many lists of competencies, characteristics, and qualities of leaders as there are companies. The literature is replete with examples. The bottom line is that your list should reflect your company's core, the beginning connection of your company's initiatives. If you have articulated a clear mission and vision, then ask what do leaders need to be able to do to help the business get there? Values speak for themselves as long as there is a commonly understood behavioral definition for each one. For example, if one of your values is quality service, what does that look like in terms of how you expect individuals in your company to behave? General value statements leave room for interpretation. The definition of values must be clear, not ambiguous.

We worked with one client as facilitators of a design team whose charter included defining a list of leadership characteristics and competencies for the organization. After researching the literature, benchmarking other organizations, and comparing this information to the core of their organization, the team decided on the following attributes: ethical, performance oriented, team builder, communicator, and change capable. Each of these attributes was defined with specific behaviors. Another client chose to use the five Exemplary Practices of Leadership, the Kouzes and Posner Leadership Challenge Model: Model the Way, Inspire a Shared Vision, Challenge the Process, Enable Others to Act, and Encourage the Heart. (www.theleadershipchallenge.com).

The list of leadership expectations that you choose should include knowledge, skills, and abilities related not only to leading oneself but also to leading others, the second part of leadership. A pivotal question each leader should be asking is, why should people follow me? Once again, if the answer is, because I do their annual evaluations, you are on the wrong track. That will get you people who will do just enough to get by and not get fired. In a word, compliance. You'll miss out on their ideas for increasing effectiveness because they will do exactly what they have been told to do and no more. It reminds me of the story of waiting in line at the airport before all the airport security checks and overhearing a conversation between a customer and a ticket agent. The customer was rude and giving the ticket agent a very difficult time. When it was my turn, I approached the counter and told the agent that I couldn't believe that the customer had given her such a hard time. She kept telling me that it was okay. After I persisted in apologizing for the customer's rude behavior, she leaned forward and whispered, "No problem. The customer is going to France, and I sent his bags to China." (Believe it or not, it still happens today.) How many of your employees are sending your bags to China because of your toxic leadership behavior?

Lastly, your list of expectations ought to include knowledge, skills, and abilities relevant to leading a successful company. This piece is the how of the Business Operating System Solution for Enterprise Results we are building with each checkpoint.

Your company must do its own homework to determine the best-fit leadership knowledge, skills, and abilities that will guide individuals in helping to achieve the vision. The list needs to answer the question, what must I, as a leader, be able to do first as a leader of self, second as a leader of others, and third as a leader of a high-performance company?

Once you have the list and have assessed yourself and your leadership team, how do you get individuals in your company to meet your expectations of them as leaders? There are three roles in leadership development whatever the size of the company:

1. The role of the company
2. The role of the leader
3. The role of the individual

First, a company's role is to create the environment in which development can happen and provide the tools for individual development. This role translates into making development a strategic priority, not an activity if you have time, and offering various types of development opportunities. Remember, classroom training is only one vehicle and not necessarily the best option. The Center for Creative Leadership published a book years ago that describes eighty-eight ways to develop leaders in place, not once mentioning seminars, conferences, or workshops (www.centerforcreativeleadership.com). This organization did a study that indicated that when leaders were asked to list the things with the most impact on how they lead, 70 percent to 90 percent listed experiences that occurred on the job.

One of the best vehicles a company can create to foster leadership development is a leadership university. Think of a leadership university not as a building but as a process of experiences that includes coaching, mentoring, shadowing opportunities, task force experiences, and temporary assignments, as well as classroom training. Even smaller companies can create these types of development opportunities. One of our clients even includes a session on what it is like to be a leader at each level. In this way individuals who think that they want to move up in the company can actually hear from someone at a higher level describe what a day in her or his life is like. Leaders often promote their best individual contributors to supervisory positions. When these people discover that their new job is really about leading people, they realize it is not what they signed up for. In addition, they often remain hands-on and frustrate their direct reports by not allowing them to do their jobs. These new leaders are trying to stay in their comfort zones of what they know and like to do.

The same is true as leaders move higher up the company ladder. One leader said to me, "If I had known there was so much politics at this level, I never would have accepted this position." How much time and money could you save with wrong selections and turnover by allowing individuals to peek into the next level of responsibility?

One of the biggest payoffs of a leadership university is the opportunity to institutionalize the knowledge, skills, abilities, and values of an effective leader at each level in the company and relate everything to the core of the business. When people understand the big picture and how people and things are connected, they can do their best work. During a conversation with an officer of a large company and another leader (one of his direct reports) about our model, the leader said she wished there were a way for everyone in the division to learn the values of and act like the officer, who was a very effective leader. A well-devised leadership development effort is the answer.

Which brings me to the second role in the leadership development process, that of the leader. As we have already stated, it is the leader's key responsibility to develop future leaders. If a company provides the environment and the tools, it is the leader's responsibility not only to allow it to happen but also to become an integral part of the process as well.

Here are some ideas:

- Internal coaching for development is about working with direct reports on specific performance issues that will help them become more effective leaders. As a supervisor, it is your job, not a responsibility you can delegate to someone else.

- Mentoring is an activity in which you choose to help someone who is not a direct report work on longer term career issues. It might be someone in your company who does not work directly with you but has the potential to become a senior leader in the future.

- External coaching requires hiring an outside expert to work with a leader in your company who may have some potential derailing behaviors or who would benefit from additional learning around specific goals to advance.

- Teaching in the leadership university is a great way to serve as a role model and to pass on your values and behaviors. You might teach a structured class around the core of your company or tell stories about your experiences. People in the company benefit from knowing what success looks and sounds like. (This approach would be an excellent vehicle for the officer of the previously mentioned company to share his effective values and behaviors.)

- The soapbox about the core is a primary responsibility for a leader. Making sure that everyone in the company knows the core, has an opportunity to define their own cores, and connect them is integral for success. When people in the company have a sense of belonging and know how they contribute, they are self-motivated to go the extra mile. They share in your passion. Too many times I hear from leaders that people at certain levels just want to do their jobs, collect their paychecks, and don't care about the big picture. My response is, just ask them. A different perspective will emerge. Yes, their survival needs are important, but if you assume that nothing else matters, you are missing tremendous performance and development opportunities.

- Model the way with your own development. While people in the organization look to their direct supervisors as the company, they look to the top to determine the definition of success. What messages are you sending? Do as I say or do as I do?

- Accountability of current leaders to develop other leaders is essential. As with other responsibilities, leaders pay attention to those things that they know they will be called upon to deliver. Just to say we must do it doesn't get you the results. Holding review meetings about leadership development in which everyone around the table is expected to report on whom they are developing and progress to date as well as embedding development of others in leaders' performance evaluations is called accountability.

The third role is that of the individual in your company. Individuals have the bottom-line responsibility for development. They must provide the willingness and the ability. Whereas the company provides the tools and the environment, and leaders provide support, individuals are the ones who must make it happen for themselves. No one can motivate anyone else. Each person must provide the self-motivation to make his or her development happen.

Self-motivation begins with willingness. Notice that I said *self*-motivation. As an aside, I am not a believer in sending people to motivational seminars. In fact, I believe leaders depend (and collectively spend millions of dollars) on such events to avoid carrying out their responsibility, which is to create an environment that allows people to be self-motivated. Individuals come back from motivational sessions with an adrenaline rush, only to find themselves in the very environment that will not support what they have learned. The rush very quickly goes away.

Willingness as defined here means "a desire to develop leadership skills." As mentioned earlier the best technicians and salespeople in companies are often promoted to leadership positions and become mediocre leaders. They would much rather have stayed in their areas of expertise but perceived up as the only way to be successful.

Once willingness is evident, the next question is, does this person have the ability to become a leader? Leadership skills are very different than technical skills. Leadership is about dealing with the gray areas of people. Just because individuals are high performers in the black and white areas of their technical competence doesn't mean that it will be so with leadership skills. In addition, companies are notorious for the sink-or-swim method of promoting people to leadership positions. "Oh, they'll learn as they go." That's a formula for disaster no matter what the level of leadership. Each level has its own skill requirements beyond its basic core competencies. Why not provide learning experiences ahead of time to avoid the potential to sink?

People in your company need to trust that you really have their best interests at heart, that you want them to succeed as leaders. This trust begins to form when you communicate the core and the related expectations of leadership to them and provide an environment that supports their development through opportunities to learn the leadership skills required for success in your company.

Passing Lane

- ☐ Leaders are the steering wheel, providing focus and direction to stay on course.

- ☐ Effective leaders build healthy, cohesive, successful, and sustainable companies.

- ☐ Your job of developing current and future leaders is key to the sustainability of your business.

- ☐ Leadership expectations should be connected to the core.

- ☐ Companies, no matter what size, need to have an effective leadership development initiative with appropriate roles defined and a variety of development opportunities.

- ☐ The creation of an effective initiative begins with the definition of your legacy, the assessment of your own abilities as well as those of your leadership team.

- ☐ Everyone, including you, should be working on a development plan so your business can drive the high performance needed to get to the next level.

Off-Road Successes

☐ Information sharing is a hallmark of effective leadership. One company holds show-me-the-money sessions that all employees are invited to attend. Company finances are openly discussed so that everyone knows where the money comes in and goes out and their impact. Even salaries, at all levels, are shared because the company strives to create an equitable environment.

☐ A fast-tech company uses a 360-degree feedback process, beginning with the CEO. He believes that the credibility of the process starts at the top. Based on the feedback the person receives from the supervisor, peers, and direct reports, the individual creates a development plan. As the individual works on the plan, the associates, who contribute to the feedback, monitor the person's behavior for the next twelve months. They note improvements on the person's performance evaluation. In the CEO's words, "Numerous miracles have been observed."

High-Performance Actions

Ready: Create

☐ Define your legacy.

☐ Define a list of leadership expectations.

☐ Assess yourself against this list.

☐ Assess members of your leadership team against this list. Ask yourself if you have the right diverse team in place.

☐ Review The BOSS Parts Inventory. Do you have a leadership development initiative that

- Supports the core and is built around the right leadership expectations?

- Starts with the hiring process?

- Provides a variety of development experiences on all levels?

- Holds leaders accountable for developing other leaders?

Set: Connect

- ☐ Is your legacy connected to the core?

- ☐ Do the expectations reflect the skills and abilities people need to work the mission, move the company toward its vision, and act on defined values?

- ☐ Does the leadership development initiative support the core?

Go: Communicate

- ☐ Is everyone in the company aware of the expectations and development opportunities as well as her or his role?

- ☐ Does each person know how all of this connects to the core?

- ☐ Is each person in your company working on a development plan?

Driving Tip

To maximize performance, expect everyone in your company to be a leader, remembering that some people are leaders of others, whereas others are leaders of self. Clarify expectations by defining what leadership means for each person in his or her job. Then provide appropriate training and development so expectations can be met.

Driving Tip

Be a great leader and role model. Spend time listening to others instead of reinforcing your own opinions.

CHECKPOINT 4:

Building Customer Loyalty

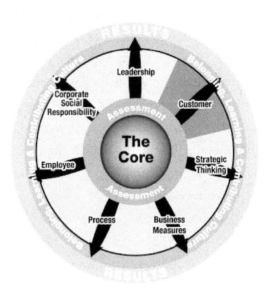

Parts Inventory

- [ ] Everyone knows who the company's customers are and who their specific customers are.

- [ ] We understand customer and stakeholder expectations.

- [ ] We have a system in place for ongoing communication with our customers and stakeholders.

- [ ] We use the customer and stakeholder data to make changes/improvements.

- [ ] Our customers and stakeholders view us as trustworthy and reliable.

- [ ] Customers and stakeholders have a high level of loyalty to our products and services.

Important Information

You are in business only as long as you have customers, people who want what you produce. This fact is true whether you produce a widget or provide a service, whether you are a for-profit, nonprofit, or not-for-profit organization. Your business requires, at least, enough customers to justify its existence. Many leaders would agree that meeting, or better yet, *exceeding* customer expectations helps to drive sustainable growth. Being out in front of your customers and anticipating their needs is the best strategy. Customers are the accelerator of your business. Retaining customers has become tougher than it was in the past as products and services become more homogeneous. A key differentiator has become the quality of customer service.

Terminology has become confusing. Different companies prefer certain references for their customer groups. Some companies use stakeholders to refer to any individual or group that has a vested interest in the success of the business. These groups typically include the board of directors, customers who use the outputs, specific individuals and groups in the surrounding community, leadership, and employees. Other companies do not consider their leadership or employees to be customer groups. Rather, they are seen as partners in serving the end users, the *real* customers. (By the way, if you don't consider your employees to be internal customers, it doesn't mean that they deserve any less respect. Having a revolving door of employees can sabotage your ability to keep your customers and stay in business. More about this topic in Checkpoint 8.)

There are many variations on this theme. Once again, the bottom line is that your company decides on a common definition of customer and ensures that it is communicated throughout the company so that everyone is on the same page.

Once you have clearly defined who constitutes your customer base, the real question becomes, does everyone in your company know who her or his specific customers are and what the customers want? On a macrolevel, you should collect customer feedback on an ongoing basis. Some businesses use surveys — mail in, electronic, and telephonic—for example. Others use face-to-face-methods, such as focus groups, and still others use a combination of methods. The importance of obtaining this feedback is to find out how you are performing relative to your customers' expectations. Too many leaders believe they know what their customers are thinking and are surprised when this feedback differs significantly from their perceptions. We tell our clients not to discount the data because they don't like it but to understand and learn from it, as difficult as that may be. It helps to create better and better results.

As part of a major transition effort, one client asked us to collect customer feedback to use as a basis for change initiatives. After determining, with the organization's leadership group, who their various customer groups were (an interesting activity in itself) and the attributes that these leaders thought were significant to their customers, we conducted telephonic surveys. Much to the leaders' dismay, some of the customers indicated they didn't know what value the organization provided. Further, *what* they were providing was not of high importance. This result was a recipe for disaster.

The first inclination of the leadership was to discount the data. According to them, it was obvious that their customers didn't have a clue. But after a cooling off period, the leaders moved forward to consider the feedback realistically and make improvements.

The moral of the story is if you want to know how your company is doing, just ask your customers. Their perceptions are your starting point. The process doesn't have to be expensive. Leaders must be involved rather than buffered from critical data. They can delegate analysis of the data but *not* the decision making with regard to what must be done in response to it. Nor can they afford to be insulated from customer interaction.

Probe and listen to the real answers. Better yet, spend some time in your customers' shoes. Answer the questions

- ○ How easy is it to do business with us?

- ○ Are we adding value?

- ○ Are we providing what the customer wants in accordance with our core, or are we giving them what we tell them they need? (The former will be the basis for your success; the latter will lead you down the wrong road.) Customer input should, at least, inform your decisions.

One note about obtaining feedback: Customers are being surveyed to death. (Think about your own experience.) The most annoying surveys are telephone calls where people halfheartedly read a script and the two minutes they told you it would take turns out to be fifteen. The second most annoying are circumstances when salespeople hand you a card to complete and tell you that their bonuses depend on your answers. Bottom line: If you are going to go to the time and expense to collect the data, make sure it is customer friendly and done well. Get back to your customers with a thank you and information about improved processes and services that resulted from their feedback. Let them know that their input counted. If you want to continue getting valuable customer data, input deserves output. It is not just a check-the-box activity.

Okay, now you know what your customers expect. Does everyone in your company know who his or her customers are? Can you and they actually deliver on expectations? An often eye-opening activity is one where each person is asked to list his or her key responsibilities, who uses the outputs of each responsibility, what each user expects, whether the users are getting what they expect, and how they know.

It's amazing, particularly in internal relationships, how often employees don't know who uses their outputs. I tell people to check with their supervisors. If they don't know, then a new question arises, why are we performing this activity?

An employee of one client followed our advice and asked his supervisor about a report he regularly supplied. He was told that a supervisor who had been gone for five years had required it and that it had taken on a life of its own. No one used it anymore. What a waste of time and resources.

All energy should be focused on the company core. If an activity or process isn't working the mission or moving the organization toward its vision, get rid of it.

Passing Lane

- You are in business only as long as you have customers.

- Customers are the accelerator, determining how fast your business grows.

- Everyone in your company should know the company's customer base as well as each of his or her own customers, whether internal or external.

- Customer input about your products and services, as well as their expectations, is the beginning of obtaining a realistic picture of the success of your company.

- Once collected, use the customer input to provide quality customer-focused service.

- All efforts from the people in your business should be focused on meeting customer expectations.

Off-Road Successes

☐ A tire-repair product company that is more than thirty years old is still going strong. One of the owners says that the secret to its success has been maintaining a solid customer base. Their strategy is to be where the customers are and to be observant— going to industry trade shows and conventions and listening to their customers when they visit their customers' shops. The owners add new products as they see what their customers are using that they don't currently provide. Socializing and getting to know the customers' families and developing trusted relationships assures that the company will continue to be the vendor of choice for their products. This customer focus will pave the road for their very successful business to be passed on to the next generation.

☐ From the beginning, a health care software company took its customer focus to heart, making it a priority to listen and learn from customers. While its customers were not always right, understanding their needs was paramount to providing the right solutions. The company's mission, to listen and learn from every client encounter, was framed and given to each new employee.

Listening to the customer also included free customer conferences. Motivational and industry experts spoke; staff and customers provided workshops on benchmark practices. A significant facet of customer focus was a customer advisory council, whose members were nominated and elected by their customer service staff. The council held face-to-face planning sessions twice a year and quarterly conference calls to discuss the product plan—what they called the good, the bad, and the ugly. As their CEO stated, "The customers told us where we needed to go. The council was an investment for us that reinforced the collaborative culture between our employees and our customers."

Finally, customers signed off on newly developed processes, a model for shared accountability. Documenting these processes allowed the company to provide predictable and consistent results and enabled the owners to sell the company when the time was right.

☐ An engineering company demonstrates a commitment to its customers by matching the local market demographics of its clients and its employees. All types of diversity issues are considered to assure that associates fit their clients, with respect to social interests, race, age, and gender. The result is that project managers and associates clearly understand their clients' perspectives and needs. Company leaders believe that being vertically integrated with their customers' benefits not only their mutual business relationship but also the community at large.

High-Performance Actions

Ready: Create

- ☐ Define your customer terminology. Who does that term include?

- ☐ Clearly identify your customer base.

- ☐ Create a process for ongoing customer feedback that directly includes the leadership and clearly defines the customers' expectations.

Set: Connect

- ☐ Does your customer base reflect what business you're in and where you want to take the company? Are you serving the right customers?

- ☐ Be certain that you can articulate to your customers what business you're in and where you are heading, most important, the added value to them.

Go: Communicate

- ☐ Ensure that everyone in your company knows who the customers are and how each individual in the company relates to the customers.

- ☐ Involve everyone in the company in creating the customer feedback process, conducting surveys and feedback sessions (when appropriate), and in making improvements based on that feedback.

Driving Tip

Have each person in your organization complete the following chart:

Key Responsibilities Of My Job	User/Customer Expectations	Performance on Expectations	How I Know

This exercise relates to both internal and external customers.

If employees don't know why something is being done or who uses the output, tell them to talk with their supervisors. If no one knows, get rid of noncore-focused activities.

If performance is not meeting expectations, explore the reasons. If there are internal obstacles, remove them, if possible, or find ways around them. Ask the user/customer for recommendations for how services may be better delivered if expectations are not being met.

CHECKPOINT 5:

Ensuring That Everyone in Your Company
Is a Strategic Thinker

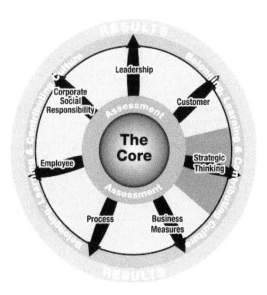

Parts Inventory

☐ Everyone in the company is a strategic thinker. Everyone considers how his or her decisions today affect tomorrow.

☐ We have developed and continuously update a strategic framework according to our customers' expectations and our mission, vision, and values.

☐ The strategic framework is cascaded down throughout the company.

☐ Leaders have articulated the strategic framework so that everyone understands how his or her objectives contribute to it.

Important Information

For a long time, companies have been operating from a very bureaucratic model of thinking and planning. It looks something like this:

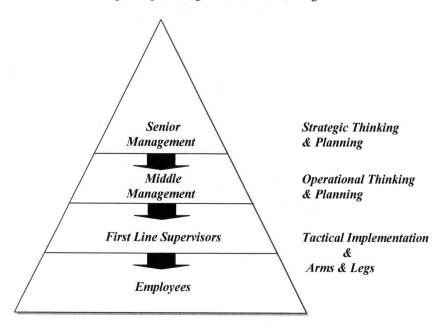

Think of this hierarchy as a person. The head does the deep thinking and long-range planning (senior leaders). The mouth articulates the high-level thinking as operational plans (middle managers). The arms and legs figure out the tactics and carry out the actions (first-line supervisors and employees). The arms and legs do not have access to the head's secret plans, so they spend a great deal of their time second-guessing how to spend their time. Time is a finite resource. No matter how successful we are, we cannot make any more time. So think of how much of it is focused on second-guessing rather than getting results.

First, with today's information overload and the ever-increasing demands of customers, this model has become obsolete. It is much too time consuming a process. The senior leaders meet to formulate the plans; the middle managers translate the plans into objectives, and then, and only then, can the first-line supervisors and employees carry out the actions as dictated by the strategic plan. This is a perfect case where small business wins out over big. Although maps are still useful, the twenty-first-century equivalent, the GPS, is faster and better.

Second, we believe that the once-a-year strategic planning and decision making model is no longer viable. It lacks the flexibility and agility that successful companies need. The only thing that is sure is change, and the pace of change is accelerating. A once–a-year devised strategic plan causes a company to miss opportunities that come along after the plan is completed. A flexible framework, based on the core of the organization, provides a foundation for fluid decision making, which focuses on the business and is able to leverage new opportunities. When you drive off road, you most often don't have a detailed map and must be able to handle surprises in the landscape as you drive.

How do you make your company a winner? By empowering everyone in your business to be a strategic thinker. You still need a strategic framework that defines your path to the future, and it still needs to cascade throughout the company so that everyone is on the same page. The defining differences are that it is not kept a secret, and everyone is held accountable for asking the following question day in and day out: how is what I am doing in my job today going to affect the company tomorrow? This question becomes increasingly more important for your company as your employees interact directly with your customers. By their tone of voice and actions, are they making it easy and desirable to do business and continue to do business with your company?

Recently we ordered chairs from a furniture company. When they arrived, the fabric was put on the wrong side up. The customer representative's solution was to offer a discount if we would keep the chairs. Do you think this person gave us a reason to want to continue doing business with this company? Was she thinking about how her solution was going to affect our future business with them(strategic thinking)? Absolutely not. Our perspective was that she just wanted to off-load the chairs (short-term thinking).

How Do You Teach People to Be Strategic Thinkers?

1. Ensure that everyone knows and has found a place in the core of your company.

2. Create, continually monitor, and update the strategic framework, whether it is a one-year, five-year, or longer plan. Remember the lesson that Alice learned from the Cheshire cat in *Alice's Adventures in Wonderland*: If you don't know where you are going, then any road will do. Because the landscape is continually changing, monitoring and updating should be an ongoing process that includes asking for input from those employees who are closest to your customers.

3. Ensure that each person's job is tied to the strategic framework and that they all understand how important their contribution is to its overall success. To emphasize this point, put the mission and vision on every performance evaluation form. Link their objectives to the overall strategies. In other words, connect the dots.

4. Teach everyone to continually ask the question, how is what I am doing in my job today going to affect the company tomorrow?

5. Hang posters with the strategic thinking question printed on them.

6. Promote accountability for this focus by including strategic thinking on performance appraisals.

Passing Lane

- ☐ The strategic framework is the GPS system, providing direction and real-time modifications.

- ☐ Every business needs a fluid document, called a strategic framework, which is monitored and updated on an ongoing basis, not just once a year as traditionally done.

- ☐ The framework should reflect the core of your business.

- ☐ Everyone in your business should be clear about how he or she contributes to the strategic framework.

- ☐ Everyone in your company should be taught the strategic thinking question, how is what I am doing in my job today going to affects the company tomorrow?

- ☐ Each person should be held accountable for the results.

Off-Road Successes

☐ It's important to stick to your knitting, but it's also necessary to move out of the box. Looking into the future, a textile company saw the proverbial handwriting on the wall. The question of what else the company could do with knitting needles morphed into a medical-products business that used its current technology to invent the first smallpox needle. The results from the initial idea were a company that developed a family of products and was eventually sold for $2 billion.

This same company realized that after the first new product went to market, the few people in the new line of business who started it didn't have the capacity to continue meeting all the business requirements themselves. Adding people would help the company move from crisis management to acting like a bigger company. To transition successfully, the company needed forward planning, including a mission statement, a clearly articulated focus and direction. Successful growth meant doing strategic planning, creating a roadmap of what to do and how to get there. Although informal, each leader presented the needs for his or her specific area; the team allocated resources and discussed direct reports. As the company moved on to the next level as planned, it developed a human resource department and formed committees so that responsibilities could be delegated.

☐ People need information to be strategic thinkers. A construction company offers "scar-tissue" classes led by the president and several executive vice presidents. In the sessions they discuss lessons they have learned from both successful and painful past work experiences. Attendees are able to learn what to do and what to *avoid* doing. The company also maintains a lessons-learned database. Project managers enter one lesson they have learned from each job to help other project managers improve their effectiveness on future assignments.

☐ Important to strategic planning is the ability to decide between yes and no. In another construction company, the strategic plan includes controlling rapid growth and making it manageable. To maintain its high-production standards, this company declines job bids if the work will require the use of external or sub-contract staff. Senior leadership has confidence in the skills of the internal staff, and this commitment to quality, the leadership believes, has earned a high percentage of repeat business.

High-Performance Actions

Ready: Create

- ☐ Ask for input in the planning process.
- ☐ Create and then monitor and update the strategic framework on an ongoing basis.

Set: Connect

- ☐ Make sure that the framework is directly connected to the core, that it reflects where you want to take the business.
- ☐ Ensure that each person's job responsibilities connect to the framework.

Go: Communicate

- ☐ Talk with or have each leader talk with her or his people to discuss how each job contributes to the strategic framework.
- ☐ Teach everyone to ask the strategic thinking question.
- ☐ Hold everyone accountable through ongoing feedback and timely performance evaluations.

Driving Tip

Even though not everyone in your company may be able to sit around the strategic planning table, create a process to get input from each person, especially those individuals most directly connected to the customer.

Driving Tip

Hold a planning session with your key leaders. It will be an eye-opening experience, especially if your team has not taken time out for thoughtful reflection. Start your planning process with a review of the core to ensure that the strategic framework will work the mission, drive toward the vision, and reflect the values. Your leaders will appreciate the time together.

CHECKPOINT 6:

Using More than Just a Rearview Mirror to Measure Success

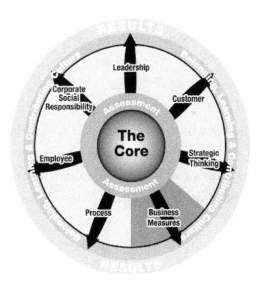

Parts Inventory

- ☐ There is a system in place to track and review company performance and capabilities, based on our strategic framework, on an ongoing basis.

- ☐ We track and review a dashboard of measures, not just financial measures.

- ☐ We are satisfied with our business results.

Important Information

Your high-performance car has a dashboard with many indicators: a gas gauge, speedometer, and oil pressure light, to name a few. These indicators alert you ahead of time if you are running out of gas, speeding, or running low on oil. They are preventative measures that give you control to rectify a pending problem. Your business should have a dashboard with these types of indicators as well. Although high-performance companies are focused on measurable results, relying on financial measures as your only indicator of success is like driving your car by looking through the rearview mirror; you get an after-the-fact look at the road behind you—too late to act if you are off course or, worse yet, veering off a cliff. What might your business dashboard look like? First , it has leading as well as lagging indicators. Lagging indicators are after-the-fact measures of success, such as return on investment and profitability, your financial metrics. Leading indicators are those measures that give you a peek into the future. They are the ones most like those on your car's dashboard. They alert you as to whether you are on course and provide opportunities to change the situation, if necessary. Examples of leading indicators include employee satisfaction, innovation, process-improvement initiatives, and customer satisfaction. (Here's a hint: Use the customer data that you've been collecting on an ongoing basis to inform your metrics.) Kaplan and Norton, in *The Balanced Scorecard*, provided an in-depth look at both types of measures. The benefits of using a dashboard are many. It translates your strategies into a measurement system that forces focus on a critical few metrics that reflect your mission and vision. The dashboard provides a focal point for communication of priorities to all employees. Once communicated, employees can determine how they contribute to the big picture, which is very self-motivating, as well as how to use their time. The leading indicators provide feedback and opportunities for learning before the finish line. The dashboard also provides a benchmark against which all new projects and potential business can be evaluated.

Having a dashboard of metrics is valuable only if you monitor it on an ongoing basis and take prompt action as required. Identifying the measures and checking them at the end of the fiscal year does nothing more than just having financial metrics. Strategic leadership means having a constant pulse on the key indicators. This monitoring can be accomplished with a software program that would provide you with line of sight throughout the business. Coupled with periodic leadership meetings, the dashboard would provide the insight you need to correct your course or celebrate successful milestones. A dashboard of metrics tailored to your business is the answer if you want to know how your customers view your products and services, what you must excel at to continue being successful, how your company can improve and continue to create value, and how you look to all your stakeholders,. Remember, the financial results are your destination, the *lagging* indicators. The *leading* indicators are your best roadmap for helping you stay on course. With all the off-road driving you need to do to be successful, wouldn't it be helpful to have indicators to alert you to the best course?

Passing Lane

☐ Effective business measures are the dashboard of your company.

☐ "I'll know it when we get there" is not a measure of business success. You have to know where "there" is. Metrics need to be put in place during the strategic planning process.

☐ You need both leading and lagging indicators of success so you can correct your course if your business is off track. Financial measures are one example of a lagging indicator, a rearview mirror approach to measuring success. Process improvement metrics, what you need to be really good at doing, is an example of a leading indicator.

☐ The metrics should be a reflection of the critical success factors of the core.

☐ Once a dashboard is developed, the key to its usefulness is the strategic leadership monitoring process.

☐ Everyone in your business should be clear about how he or she is connected to the company's metrics and all should be held accountable for their contributions.

Off-Road Successes

- ☐ The president of an engineering firm has a dashboard of measures he tracks throughout the year that serves as an early-warning system. It includes measures such as meeting commitments on projects, developing new skills, delivering products and services, as well as financial metrics. A software program developed in-house gives him easy access and line of sight up, down, and throughout the firm.

- ☐ Another company tracks its internal-customer-service satisfaction through a feedback database. Each time a department provides services to another, a satisfaction survey is included. The human resource director said that the result is a continuous innovation process and high-satisfaction levels.

- ☐ A third example is a company that has developed metrics to measure employees' enthusiasm to determine their level of satisfaction. Key indicators include the number of people willing to take on challenging assignments and the number who take on business opportunities in other geographic locations. The result is an ongoing heads-up about employee satisfaction and the company's ability to meet client needs.

High-Performance Actions

Ready: Create

- ☐ Identify what indicators you would look at to determine how you are doing financially; how satisfied your customers are; if your internal processes are working well; if you are continually adding value; and if you are getting better through improvement and innovation.

- ☐ Create the process for ongoing monitoring of your dashboard, including who is involved in the process.

Set: Connect

- ☐ How do these measures relate to the core of your business?

- ☐ How are they reflected in your strategic framework?

- ☐ How do these measures show up in each person's performance expectations and feedback?

Go: Communicate

- ☐ Once you have created your dashboard, with the help of the appropriate people, ensure that each person in your company has the opportunity to discuss your expectations of her or him based on how that person contributes to these metrics.

Driving Tip

Select only a few critical measures of success. Measuring everything is oppressive and counterproductive. Although each person's job metrics may not be the same, they should cascade up to your company's measures of success.

CHECKPOINT 7:

Continually Innovating and Improving Your Processes to Keep Pace with Your Customers' Demands

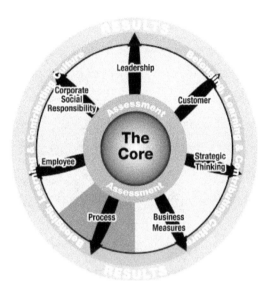

Parts Inventory

☐ We have all the technology, facilities, and equipment that we need to excel.

☐ Our processes are clearly defined.

☐ Our processes are customer focused.

☐ Our processes are defined so that our employees are able to do their best work.

☐ The company has a process in place for continuous improvement and innovation based on customers' expectations.

Important Information

Key business processes are ones that people in a company must excel at to satisfy customers and other stakeholders. Quickly, name the three to five key processes of your company. Our experience has been that most leaders cannot identify these critical processes or document how they are done. Just like a car manual, a company should also have a manual that explains how things work. Documenting is important so that

1. You have a baseline look at how to continuously improve or innovate by identifying where things are falling through the cracks

2. When new employees come on board, they are able to go up the learning curve much more quickly rather than guess how you want things done

3. The processes are performed consistently, regardless of who is involved, and are not employee dependent

4. If you grow beyond one location, the processes are repeatable when you are not there to direct them

   (Have you ever called three different people in the customer service center of a company trying to resolve the same problem? Point made.)

Some examples of key processes (not necessarily yours) are the sales process, the inventory process, the billing process, the troubleshooting process, and the product and service delivery process. Other examples include the leadership-development process, the knowledge-management process, and the financial-management process. Processes should be customer focused and employee enabled. Start by looking at the process through your customers' (both internal and external) eyes and understanding their expectations. Then create the process so that employees are able to do their best work.

The process for creating and documenting processes (yes, there's a process for everything) is not difficult. It works in businesses of all sizes. It takes the right people, the right steps, and a time commitment. The time commitment will provide a return on investment many times over. Notice we have used the terms *improvement* as well as *innovation*. You want to avoid the trap of getting better and better at doing the wrong thing. For example, Kodak spent time improving the process of making chemical film when it should have been focusing on digital technology. What are you trying to improve that may be old school?

For each process design, there should be a team of individuals that includes people who currently work in the process, customers of the process (if it is an internal process; some companies do include external customers, as well), and people with creative fresh eyes who don't work in the process. The process steps are

1. Review the core of your organization.
2. Document the current process as it is now being done.
3. Identify what is working and what is not working according to the team.
4. Survey or interview customers of the process to identify their expectations and notions of what is working and not working.
5. Compare the feedback with the team information.
6. Benchmark companies in and outside of your industry who excel at the process.
7. Determine what would work to improve the process in your company, including technology, equipment, and facility requirements. (Is innovation rather than improvement needed?)
8. Design the new process.

One of the common issues we run across with existing processes is that too many hands are in the process, which allows for too many opportunities for things to fall through the cracks. Figuring out who owns the process, the person ultimately responsible and accountable, and the details of how the work should be divided are essential next steps.

One of our clients decided to design its processes by putting "the smart people" (aka leadership) in a room to figure them out. Several months later we were called in to create a new initiative for process design using their employees, the people closest to the customers, and those people involved in the processes. Do it right the first time so you don't have to do it over. Using employees creates tremendous buy in for the results. Having a process for continuous improvement and innovation responds to customer demand for faster, better, and more cost-effective products and services.

One more important note. Process needs should drive technology, not vice versa. Implementing the latest and greatest technology before defining the objectives and criteria of the process results in very expensive technologies with little return on investment.

Two examples come to mind. The first is an organization wanting to improve its performance evaluation system. The staff bought a software program before understanding what was wanted from the new process. The result was an automated system that met nobody's needs. Second is a company with multiple locations that identified a need for an information-management process. Again, the company bought an expensive software program that addressed the symptoms but left the underlying causes of the issue unresolved.

One common concern is lack of control by leadership. Any process-design initiative should be defined with regularly scheduled meetings along the way for teams to report to leadership on their progress. We call them reconciliation meetings. Leaders should be careful not to stifle creativity but, in the end, serve as a reality check when it comes to available resources to implement changes inherent in the processes.

Passing Lane

☐ Processes are the part of the car manual that explains how things work.

☐ High-performance companies are focused not only on results but also on how they get to those results.

☐ You should be able to identify and document your key business processes, the critical few things that your company must be great at doing to be successful.

☐ It is important to document them so that they can be performed consistently, they are repeatable, a new employee can move up the learning curve more quickly, and you have a baseline from which to continuously improve and innovate.

☐ Processes should be customer focused and designed so that employees can do their best work.

☐ There is a process for documenting and improving as well as innovating key processes that includes utilizing employees. This process is especially important for buy in.

Off-Road Successes

☐ One young business began rather quickly with little thought to its organization and processes. Although it was part of a larger entity, it had its own mission. After several years of functioning, a new leader took over the key position and recognized the need to take a hard look at how the business was organized.

We worked with the leadership team to validate the mission, vision, and values (always a first step). Then, together, we identified the key processes. After gathering employee and customer feedback, the team recognized that the clear message was that it was not easy to do business with their organization nor were the processes defined in a way that allowed employees to do their best work. Using employee teams and the steps described in this checkpoint, the five key processes were documented and improved to meet customer and employee needs. A positive by-product, as reported by a member of the leadership team, is that the employees now use what they learned in this process to improve their work every day.

☐ Another example comes from the nonprofit world. An organization with a very small staff that greatly depends upon its volunteers to accomplish its work found the external and internal environmental conditions dramatically changing. The organization was in transition; it was looking for a new executive director and staff members were trying to be all things to all people. Because they were overwhelmed, the result was high turnover. Traditional members/volunteers felt left behind, and the deterioration in timely responses to member needs was unacceptable.

A transition team was appointed. The team became educated on the process and, in turn, educated the board of directors on the need and the plan. The core was clearly defined.

Existing customer feedback was scrutinized to identify priority issues. Subteams were formed, key processes were documented and improved according to the feedback, and processes and resources were aligned with the new strategic plan. The process teams identified quick fixes for short-term success.

Since then, the organization has become focused on its members' needs and expectations with processes that allow its staff to do its best work. Now the organization also has the capacity to continuously improve to stay ahead of the customer expectation curve.

High-Performance Actions

Ready: Create

- ☐ Identify your key processes, what you must excel at to be successful.

Set: Connect

- ☐ Check to ensure that these processes are critical to your mission and vision and are designed with company values in mind.

- ☐ Check against the strategic framework. Do these processes reflect and support your strategies?

Go: Communicate

- ☐ Provide employees with documentation of their processes ensuring that they understand the customer focus and are able to do their best work.

- ☐ To improve processes, identify and charter (explain the task and the parameters) employee process teams. Ensure that they have the right team leadership and authority to do their work, including time, money, and accessibility to others within the company and to customers, as well as authority to benchmark best practices outside the company. Identify milestone communication points between the teams and leadership.

Driving Tip

Michael Hammer, author of *Reengineering the Corporation,* said that putting smart people in stupid processes makes them stupid. Continuously innovate and improve your processes so they are not stupid. Leverage the talents of your people; don't handicap them.

CHECKPOINT 8:

Attracting, Developing, and Retaining Top-Notch Employees

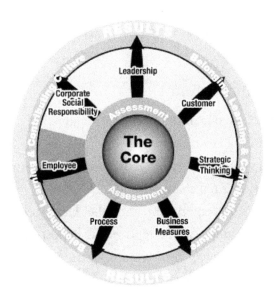

Parts Inventory

☐ We have defined the skills, abilities, and culture-fit priorities our company needs for success based on our mission, vision, and values.

☐ We hire according to these established needs.

☐ We are able to attract and retain the people we need.

☐ Each employee has individual and team performance objectives that directly relate and contribute to the desired results defined in the strategic framework.

☐ We have a system in place for ongoing two-way communication with our employees.

- Company and job-relevant information is readily available to our employees.

- There is a system in place for providing ongoing feedback to employees on performance.

- People in the company are rewarded for their performance based on their objectives (individual, team, and company).

Important Information

"Our employees are our most important resource." If I had a dollar for every time I heard a key leader say those words and then treat people as expendable cogs in a wheel, I'd be on my way to a comfortable retirement. Lou Gerstner, Jr., retired chairman and CEO of IBM, said that he could lose the buildings, the equipment, and other hard resources and survive because all those things can be replaced. If he lost the employees, the business could not survive. Furthermore, Gerstner stated that, at the end of the day, your company is nothing more than the collective capacity of your employees to create value. Your employees are the fuel that enables your high-performance company to exceed expectations on your off-road journey.

Attracting and retaining top-notch employees is getting more difficult. It's one of the chief concerns of most leaders. And it should be. A Bureau of Labor report indicated that by 2010, there would be 10 million more jobs than there are people to fill them. You need to attract and retain people who can move your company beyond what you can do alone. It becomes more and more important as you ratchet up to the next level. A 2005 Spherion Emerging Workforce Study (www.spherion.com), still applicable today, indicated that

- More than one half of employees are very likely to look for a new work situation.

- ☐ Almost three-quarters of employees say they will look for a new job at their own initiative.

- ☐ Almost one-half of employees want to change jobs every three to five years, even if at the same company.

- ☐ However, people believe they have more growth potential if they leave their current companies.

- ☐ Workers no longer see changing jobs as potentially harmful to career success.

The statistics and timing may vary, but even in a down economy, employees are still loyal to their careers, not necessarily to the organizations.

You have your job cut out for you. To attract the right employees, you must start the process before the search. You have to define the skills and abilities the business needs based on the core. You need not only people who can work your mission and help your company achieve its vision but also individuals who share the values of the business and fit into the culture. More turnover is caused by a person-culture misfit than by a lack of skills and abilities. Remember the example from Checkpoint 3, the human resource director the small business client hired from a very large company? She was used to a large budget and staff. Nowhere in the interview process was the difference in the cultures addressed. She was walking into a hands-on job with little budget and no staff, except for a shared assistant. Of course, she became a turnover statistic. The moral of the story is that you need not only to clearly define the skills and abilities for the position but also to create questions around the culture of your company. Then hire according to those needs and culture fit.

Once hired, the retention process begins the first day the employee arrives. There are two types of initial processes that build retention: the onboarding process, which is designed to jump-start relationship building and provide formal and informal knowledge of the company culture, and the orientation process, which is more administrative in nature, such as the completion of payroll and benefits paperwork. Each person should understand the lay of the land of the company as well as the specifics of the job. Assigning a buddy who can explain to the new employee the way things are organized and done in the company is helpful. An individual's supervisor or you (if you don't have layers of leaders) need to clarify the job, discuss expectations, establish objectives, and walk through the performance feedback process. One president of a company immediately assigns a new employee to a committee. The assignment serves two purposes: It gets the employee involved right away, meeting others, and the employee comes with fresh eyes to help solve a company issue.

Retaining employees and creating self-motivation is critical to getting to the next level of success. Here's where it gets interesting. There are four generations in the workplace today, each with its own set of motivators. Morris Massey wrote about this very issue years ago in his work *What You Are Is Where You Were When ...* (out of print). He said that our values are a product of the times in which we grew up. For example, the veterans (1928–1945) were impacted by the Depression, so they value highly having a roof over their heads and food on their tables. The veterans are very loyal, respect authority, and get satisfaction from a job well done. Many in this group are being hired back on a part-time basis. What motivates this group is knowing that their experience is respected, giving input on what has and has not worked in the past, valuing their perseverance, and receiving personal notes and plaques as recognition of work well done. They make great mentors to the younger generations, and this role is a good way to recognize their wisdom and experience.

The baby boomers (1946–1964) are service oriented. Many grew up as the "have" generation. They had a roof over their heads and food on their tables, so they are looking for meaningful work. They are driven, so they are willing to go the extra mile. The boomers are good at relationships, are good team players, and want to please. Motivators for this generation include letting them know that their hard work and long hours are valued, their contributions are unique and important, your approval, and public recognition, including perks.

Gen Xers (1965–1979) are the first generation to grow up in the technology age, so they are technoliterate. They are attracted by leading-edge technology. They are adaptable, independent, and, unlike their predecessors, not intimidated by authority. Gen Xers are not very corporate and would rather work in a place with few rules. They want control over their work, including the freedom to operate, which often translates into, I can do this work at home. Why do I need to have face time at the office? They can work on concurrent projects and want plenty of constructive feedback.

The Millenials/Gen Y (1980–2000) are different still. They tend to be optimistic and tenacious, to have multitasking capability, to be more technologically savvy than Gen Xers and to like collective action. They are goal oriented and impatient to make it. The Millenials are motivated by working with other bright individuals, especially creative people. They like to believe that they can help turn the company around or help take it to the next level, heroic action. They like being mentored by older more experienced people, coupled with training and development.

In the end analysis, some universal motivators are discussed in Checkpoint #10. The bottom line? *All employees need to trust that you have their best interests in mind.*

A key retention factor is the alignment of an individual's career goals with the company's goals. Following that, individuals want to be associated with a winning team and believe that things will be great by working for a great company. Just ask the employees of FORTUNE magazine's 100 Best Companies to Work For, or refer to Jim Collins' examples in his book *Good to Great*. Additionally, two-way ongoing communication is essential for high performance. Employees need to know not only your expectations of them and how they are doing relative to those expectations but also the big business picture and where they fit in, how they contribute. Lastly, when they meet your expectations, employees need to know that their contributions matter and are appreciated. Recognition gives people pride in their work. Jon Katzenbach, in his book *Why Pride Matters More Than Money*, stated that pride is the powerful motivating force that builds long-term sustainability of companies; it drives people to go the extra mile for high performance. Other authors refer to this practice as getting ordinary people to do extraordinary things. No matter the generation, people want to be treated like adults. And when treated as such, in most cases, they become self-motivated high performers.

Reward for contributions are important not only on the individual level but also on the team level. Racecar teams represent some of the best high-performance teams. Each member knows his or her job, understands the criticality of performing well (especially under pressure), and gets rewarded not only on individual performance but also on team performance. Everyone is key for success. The teams in your company are no different.

One last thought about recognition. Recognition comes in many forms, and different people like to be recognized in different ways. The wrong venue for recognition can be punishing instead of rewarding. Although we have generational clues that are generalizations, people are still individual. Some people like large group recognition (i.e., employee banquets, all-hands-on-deck meetings); others find that embarrassing. Still others like to be rewarded within their own work group, and some find that recognition promotes jealousy among co-workers. Many like one-on-one recognition (i.e., a note from you, be taken to lunch). What these differences mean is that you need to get to know your employees.

Passing Lane

- [ ] Employees are your most important resource. They are the fuel that powers your high-performance company.

- [ ] Talented employees are becoming more difficult to find.

- [ ] Attracting and retaining top-notch employees begins before the search with defining not only job specifications but also company-culture specifications.

- [ ] Retaining valued employees starts the first day on the job and continues throughout the duration of employment.

- [ ] Initial and ongoing communication about job-specific information, performance feedback, and general big-picture company information is critical for high performance.

- [ ] Explain your expectations, coach along the way providing positive and negative feedback, and reward commensurate with meeting your expectations.

- [ ] The multiple generations of workers makes it more difficult to lead. You need to understand the different work styles and motivators for each generation.

- [ ] Regardless of generation, employees want to know that they can trust that leaders have their best interests in mind, to believe that they are working for a great company, to know that there is open two-way communication, and to have pride in their work and the company.

Off-Road Successes

☐ One fast-tech company CEO believes in the balance of meaningful work with quality personal time. He said that this accommodating philosophy has helped him retain a talented and frequently recruited senior leader. With two young children, this leader left a higher paying position with longer hours to work at this firm. Similarly, this company offers flexdays and teleworking options for employees. With these options, employees are able to adjust their workdays around personal schedules and family responsibilities. Turnover is very low in this organization.

☐ The medical technology company from Checkpoint 5 was in a fast-growth mode. Communication was the biggest hurdle. The first step taken was to make everyone computer savvy. Other strategies for effective communication included lots of memos and companywide quarterly face-to-face meetings. The challenge was to balance face-to-face meetings without taking over getting the business done.

Although the company grew to more than 4,000 people, it retained a family atmosphere. The company had one of the lowest turnover rates in the industry because of its focus on people. There was a conscious effort to accommodate work-life balance. The leaders were sensitive to the fact that they took their salespeople away from their families for conferences; however, training salespeople was a top priority. One month before each conference, the president sent a letter and a gift each week to spouses thanking then for their support, recognizing that they were going to be left behind. One executive said that the highlight of her career was bringing in great people, helping them develop a successful career, carrying the corporate flag, and treating people with dignity and respect.

High-Performance Actions

Ready: Create

- ☐ Create a high-performance employee system that includes
  - ○ Well-thought-out questions for the interviewing process based on needed skills and abilities as well as culture fit
  - ○ A way to integrate new employees into the company
  - ○ An expectation setting discussion based on job-specific as well as general company information
  - ○ A process for ongoing, two-way communication about performance and big-picture information
  - ○ A reward system commensurate with individual, team, and company performance

Set: Connect

- ☐ Make sure that the skills and abilities you require are directly tied to the core of your business and support the strategic framework.

Go: Communicate

- ☐ Hold a discussion with employees to talk about the core of the business and the expected value-related behaviors.
- ☐ Discuss the company's customer base and the employee-specific customers.
- ☐ Relate employees' job contributions to the strategic framework, including individual performance-related metrics.
- ☐ Provide documentation of the processes in which the employees will be working.
- ☐ Discuss the two-way communication process, including how and when the employees will receive feedback on performance as well as general company information.

Driving Tip

Use your current employees to help develop the culture-fit questions for the interview process. Ask them to identify, aside from skills and abilities, what it takes to succeed in the company.

Driving Tip

Put the mission and vision on the cover page of all performance evaluations to remind people in your company that they are all working toward the same goal. Include values, translated into behaviors, as part of the performance review for everyone. This action reinforces that the means are as important as the end.

CHECKPOINT 9:

Leaving Small and Big Company Tire Tracks

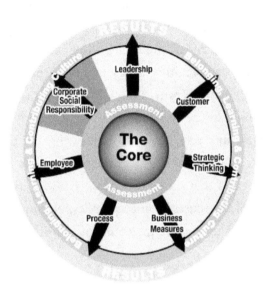

Parts Inventory

☐ We increase the size of our social and economic tire track by participating in activities that support the surrounding communities in which we operate.

☐ Our company and its processes are designed to decrease the environmental tire track we leave on the earth's resources.

Important Information

Just as many of us are redefining high performance for our cars as we are watching gas prices soar, learning more about the effects of emissions on the earth, becoming more attuned to carpooling, and driving in the HOV lane, so should we be doing the same for our business. What are we taking from the earth to use in our processes? What and where is the waste when we are done? The fact of the matter is the earth is a closed system, so when we say the waste goes somewhere, that somewhere is right here.

Identify one of your key processes used in the production of your products or services. Trace the inputs, the throughputs, and outputs. I think you will be surprised at how many resources you are using up and the amount of waste at the back end of the process. Even if you identify a process that is fairly clean, you'll be surprised at what else is being wasted in your company. One CEO of a company sent around an e-mail stating that the company was no longer buying paper clips. The results were amazing. Instead of throwing the clips away after one use, people in his company used them repeatedly. Why not? The results were so good that the next e-mail was about rubber bands and so on through all the reusable office supplies. Not only was it a small-tire-track step to take, it saved the company considerable money in its office supply account.

One hero in leaving a small company tire track is Ray Anderson, founder of InterfaceFLOR in Atlanta, Georgia, and a pioneer in the worldwide effort of sustainable development. Ray was concerned about what state the earth would be in for his grandchildren—the legacy we will leave—and decided to embark on a journey to sustainability in his company. His mission became that his would be the first business that showed the industrial world, through actions, what all the dimensions of sustainability looked like, including people, processes, products, place, and profits. InterfaceFLOR is learning to harness green energy, to provide raw materials by harvesting and recycling, and to eliminate harmful waste. Its solutions are practical, creative, and profitable. InterfaceFLOR's sustainability mission is mission zero—first sustainable, then restorative. It's pretty amazing for a flooring company.

If you're saying that you will comply with government regulations, what you are *really* saying is that you are being as bad as the law allows. Think about elevating it to sustainability, meeting the needs of the present without compromising the ability of future generations to meet their own needs. Or better yet, ratchet it up one more level to restorative, which means putting back more than you take, doing good as well as doing no harm.

Hotels represent an industry that is also taking the lead in the green movement. The Orchard Garden in the Financial District in San Francisco was built to the standards developed by the U.S. Green Building Council. The hotel began asking guests to conserve water by not having towels and linens changed each day, installing low-flow commodes and showerheads, and purchasing and using nontoxic cleaning supplies. The Habitat Suites Hotel in Austin, Texas, uses solar hot-water systems. It has cut its natural gas consumption by 60 percent. The Lenox Hotel in Boston, Massachusetts, composts 120 tons of restaurant waste per year. The Las Vegas Mirage is building green and getting a tax write-off, not to mention saving money on power bills and other related utilities.

The large tire track is the flip side of being a good steward of the earth's resources (small tire track). This tire track has everything to do with recognizing that your business is part of a community system. You won't get to the next level of success without becoming part of the community in which you operate. How do you give back? Do you provide time for your employees to perform volunteer work? (By the way, some of the best learning experience for development is accomplished through volunteer assignments.) Do you partner with a school for tutoring, mentoring, or making presentations for career day? Which community organizations do you financially support? There are endless ways you and your business can give to the community.

Passing Lane

- ☐ Corporate social responsibility is the equivalent of carpooling, saving the earth's resources and including others.

- ☐ Corporate social responsibility is a critical performance area for every company because high-performance success doesn't come in isolation from the community system in which it operates.

- ☐ Leaving a small tire track means figuring out how your business can make itself less economically dependent on resources or practices that have no future use.

- ☐ Leaving a large tire track translates into giving back to the community in which your business operates in the forms of volunteering or financial support, for example.

Off-Road Successes

You are never too small to leave a big tire track. A home remodeling company with fewer than twenty employees has found its niche in the competitive world of construction. The CEO prides himself on his company's ability to remodel a kitchen or bath within three and one-half weeks, and he's working on cutting that time down. How can this schedule be possible? He attributes the company's success to his permanent employees and the respect with which they are treated. The employees have steady work and all the materials they need for the job. Their opinions count. The company's overall turnover is one-half the industry average also because of his partner's having a background in human resources and hiring right. Being small hasn't stopped this company from being involved in the community. The CEO said that his employees volunteer to help complete home repairs for senior citizens. Joining forces with Rebuilding Together is the company's way of supporting the community in which it operates.

High-Performance Actions

Ready: Create

- ☐ Create your company's small tire track with these questions in mind:
  - ○ What is the legacy you want your company to leave?

  - ○ What is the strategy to prosper as you become a sustainable company?

  - ○ What if everything that came into your company could not be discarded? How would you design your processes and procedures?

  - ○ How can you design your company's processes so that you maximize the efficiency of resources used?

  - ○ After answering these questions, review and ask: Are we systematically making ourselves less economically dependent on resources that have no future use, cannot be recycled?

- ☐ Decide how your company will connect to the surrounding community. How will it affect the business?

Set: Connect

- ☐ Connect the small and large tire tracks to the core of your company.

- ☐ Make corporate social responsibility a leadership responsibility for everyone in your company, and hold them accountable through the feedback you provide.

- ☐ Include corporate social responsibility as a key result area in your strategic framework with the appropriate metrics.

- ☐ Conduct a small- tire-track check on all your processes.

Go: *Communicate*

☐ Hold discussions with everyone in your company to educate them about corporate social responsibility, the company's strategy, and everyone's roles.

☐ Provide continuous feedback about how the company is performing relative to the metrics, as well as how each employee is meeting expectations related to corporate social responsibility.

Driving Tip

There are four potential levels of a small tire track. Start where you are comfortable.

> **Level 1:** Reuse office supplies. Use earth-friendly maintenance supplies. Recycle.
>
> **Level 2:** Treat your employees as a valuable resource, nonexpendable versus expendable. Watch for burnout.
>
> **Level 3:** Review your current processes. Identify ways to minimize use of nonrenewable resources as well as waste.
>
> **Level 4:** As you decide on new lines of business or business processes, create them at the restorative level. If you are constructing a building, build it as green as possible and with its destruction in mind. What will be the waste versus the reuse?

CHECKPOINT 10:
Creating a BLC Culture for
Sustainability of Your Company

Parts Inventory

- ☐ Our leaders have created a culture in which employees want to belong.

- ☐ Our leaders have created a culture in which employees want to continuously learn.

- ☐ Our leaders have created a culture in which employees want to contribute to the success of the business.

Important Information

Driving off road certainly has its challenges: no paved roads, no roadmap, and unanticipated obstacles, to name a few. A high-performance car doesn't eliminate any of these potential problems, but a well-tuned one can make the drive more worry free and productive. Similarly, a well-tuned business operating within the right culture can make the difference between moderate and great success. Do you want to know the real culture of your company? Just ask your employees two simple questions: Why would they recommend to a best friend to come work in your company? Why not? The answers will be very revealing. Those businesses that create a culture in which people want to come (as well as recommend that their best friends join), develop, and stay will be the winners. As previously discussed, talented employees are becoming more difficult to find and keep, so your company culture has become more important as a competitive edge. You need a BLC culture.

No, I didn't misspell BLT, as in the sandwich. Whatever generation, you need great people to work your strategies and help you achieve your goals. Creating a BLC culture can do just that. Remember, as we mentioned in Checkpoint 8, Louis Gerstner, retired CEO of IBM said that an organization is nothing more than the collective capacity of its people to create value.

What is a BLC culture? It is a culture in a company in which people want to belong, learn, and contribute to the success of the business. It is the net result of implementing the Business Operating System Solution for Enterprise Results. Remember, the BOSS connects all the checkpoints to the core of your organization (its mission, vision, and values) and to each other.

Once the connections are made and communicated using the process we've discussed in this book, the real work of the BLC culture can begin. It is worth reiterating here the importance of giving individuals in your business the time and direction to connect their own cores with that of the company's. It gives meaning to the work they do and empowers them to go the extra mile.

So what does BLC really mean, and what are some actionable steps that you can take beyond creating, connecting, and communicating initiatives using the BOSS? Everyone wants a sense of belonging; that's why we belong to families and civic and religious organizations. It's why many people, just like the individuals in your business who chose to come to work for you, work for companies. Here are some steps you can take to create a culture of belonging:

☐ The first day employees show up for work, have someone there to greet them, introduce them to others, and give them the lay of the land. ("Hi, and here's your work area" doesn't count.)

☐ Each morning when you see an employee, say good morning. (You'd be surprised how many people tell us their boss doesn't acknowledge their presence.) Make sure employees understand their roles and responsibilities as well as your expectations. (Handing them a job description doesn't qualify as achieving this action item.)

☐ Sponsor business functions that include employees' families. (Make them voluntary because some employees would rather spend their time away from work—away from work *people*.)

☐ Provide business logo items to employees, such as memo pads, coffee mugs, shirts.

Everyone wants to continue to learn, grow, and develop. In these fast-changing times, you can't afford not to. Even if you stay in the same position for years, requirements of the job will keep changing, and you must change just to keep up. From a company standpoint, customers want higher quality and faster and more cost-effective products and services, which translates into employees producing higher quality products and services more effectively and efficiently. That requires continuous learning. Remember the definition of *insanity*: "doing the same thing over and over again and expecting different results." Here are some actions for providing a learning culture:

- □ Continually provide feedback on performance to employees. (Saving it up for the surprise end-of-the-year performance evaluation is counterproductive.)

- □ Sending employees to training is only one way to develop people (and not always the best way). Consider coaching, shadowing, temporary assignments, and participation on problem-solving teams.

- □ Pass on articles of interest in professional and trade journals.

- □ Delegate one of your responsibilities that has become routine to you but that would be new and challenging to your employee.

- □ After returning from a learning experience, ask the person to teach others who would also like to learn. (And what a great return on your investment.)

Lastly, all employees want to know that their coming to work every day makes a difference. They develop pride in knowing that they have contributed to helping the company achieve its goals and move toward its vision. Below are some ways that you can provide a sense of contribution:

- □ Articulate clearly how the individual contributes to the success of the business. ("Here is how what you do matters.") And then do it over and over again as they continue contributing.

- □ Thank people for a job well done. (An attitude of "why should I thank them; they get paid to do their jobs" gets you compliance. It buys you arms and legs, not people who want to go the extra mile.)

- □ Give timely, well-thought-out performance evaluations. (The message you send to your employees when evaluations are not timely and well thought out is that they are not a high priority for you. Just think about how important feedback on your performance is to you.)

☐ When individuals go the extra mile, write a personal note to them, take them to lunch, put a memo in their personnel file, recognize them at a staff meeting, present them with a certificate—just to name a few ways. (Remember personal likes and dislikes about being rewarded.)

In summary, to create a BLC culture, first make sure that you have designed your Business Operating System Solution for Enterprise Results so that it connects all initiatives you have in place and those you are yet to develop; that it enables communication across the business and that it couples individuals' cores with the company's core. Then, it's on to actionable steps to implement ways of belonging, learning, and contributing that enable you to attract, develop, and retain top-notch people who will help you achieve your goals and create value. Build a culture of success, and people will stay and drive high performance. It's smart business.

Passing Lane

☐ A well-tuned business infrastructure, using the BOSS model, operating within the right culture can be the difference between moderate and great results.

☐ You need to create a BLC culture to attract and retain the talent that will get you high-performance results.

☐ Everyone wants a sense of belonging.

☐ Everyone wants to continue to learn, grow, and develop.

☐ Everyone wants to know that his or her showing up every day makes a difference, that his or her contributions count.

Off-Road Success

Becoming a BLC Culture

This visionary leader realized that his organization was not positioned to succeed in the twenty-first-century competitive environment, and so he put together a team of key leaders and tasked them with determining the right approach to get to the next level of success. The team interviewed multiple consulting firms and hired us to guide them through the change. We were people who could get them out of their comfort zones because we were unfamiliar with their industry.

This team morphed into the leadership team that drove the process. Initially, the team became educated about the process; confirmed its mission, vision, and values; and coordinated a comprehensive assessment including employees and customers. Then, employing existing assessment data and the new results, the leadership team identified the top five priorities that needed to be addressed to get the organization to where it needed to be.

Internal teams were chartered, each with a specific priority, to document current processes, benchmark state-of-the-art practices inside and outside the industry, and recommend the best way to serve customers and enable employees to do their best work. Team membership was determined with the purpose of not only completing the task at hand but also creating long-lasting working relationships. The focus was on sharing instead of duplicating resources, streamlining, and leveraging technology.

No stone was left unturned. The leadership team continued to learn about leading change and strategic leadership. The internal teams learned more than they ever could have imagined and had a tremendous sense of contribution. All participants were recognized and rewarded for going the extra mile.

The result was an organization ready to compete in the twenty-first-century competitive environment. Are they perfect? Not yet. There is always room for continuous improvement and innovation. Have they reached the next level of success? Absolutely, as evidenced by their becoming a role model for other organizations and succeeding in meeting their recruiting needs while others in their industry have suffered.

High-Performance Actions

Ready: Create

- [ ] Conduct a culture audit of your company using The BOSS Scheduled Maintenance Checkup. Add some open-ended questions, such as
  - What should we stop doing?
  - What should we start doing?
  - What should we continue doing?
  - What is one change you would implement to make this company a better place to work?

- [ ] Using responses to the audit, determine what you need to stop doing, start doing, keep on doing, and changes you need to implement to become a BLC culture.

- [ ] Continually reassess your company for lasting success.

Set: Connect

- [ ] Ensure that anything you implement is consistent with the core and other infrastructure initiatives.

Go: Communicate

- [ ] Discuss the results of The BOSS Scheduled Maintenance Checkup with your employees, including
  - Feedback about what to stop, start, and continue
  - Priority changes that will be made
  - Any suggested changes that were frequently mentioned but cannot be done, and why

Driving Tip

Ask employees

- ☐ What attracted them to your company?

- ☐ What keeps them there?

- ☐ What gets in their way of high performance?

Continue to act on the positive feedback.
Address the obstacles to high performance.

Summary: Troubleshooting Matrix

The first step is always to make sure that the symptom is not related to the lack of connection to the core or to the lack of communication throughout the company.

Then check:

Symptom	Possible Cause	Solution
Persistent problems	Treating symptoms; not getting to the root of the issues	Using an objective facilitator, administer the BOSS Maintenance Inventory and follow up with focus groups.
People in the company heading in different directions	No clearly defined core; core not communicated throughout the company or no accountability to stick to the core	Define the core and clearly communicate to all, allowing each person to find the connection.
Lack of ROI on strategies, activities, and so forth	No connection to the core	Reevaluate whether each is working the mission, moving you toward the vision and acting on the values. Eliminate or create an exit strategy for those that are not connected and are draining resources.
High turnover	Poor leadership practices	Implement a leadership development process that is connected to the core and hold leaders accountable for acting on these practices.

Symptom	*Possible Cause*	*Solution*
No leader replacements	No pool of ready leaders	Implement a leadership development process and develop potential leaders ahead of time.
Customer turnover	Not meeting customer expectations	Create and implement a customer-feedback process. Use the feedback in improving company products, services, and processes.
Employees disengaged and customer complaints	No understanding by frontline employees of the impact they have on customers; or disgruntled employees	Teach employees to ask the strategic thinking question. Hold focus groups to get employees' feedback and act on what's possible to change.
Crisis management	No forward planning	Create and implement a strategic framework, including developing or improving the infrastructure.
Lack of focus on what's truly important to measure	Oppressive number of metrics or everything is a priority	Create a balanced dashboard of metrics that are truly significant to your business success, including both leading and lagging indicators.
Not meeting targets	No leading indicators	Identify significant leading indicators and monitor continually. Course correct as needed.

Symptom	*Possible Cause*	*Solution*
Customers and employees leaving	Poor processes	Get feedback. Implement a continuous improvement plan to create customer-focused and employee-enabled processes.
Lack of ability to attract or retain the right people	Toxic environment	Create a BLC culture by administering The BOSS Parts Inventory and acting on the priority issues. Hold leaders accountable for effective leadership practices.
Excess waste with perceived unnecessary expenditures	Lack of emphasis on conserving resources	Review the four levels of a small tire track, and start implementing at the appropriate level.
Employees feeling disconnected from the community	Lack of philanthropic activities	Create a process, with employees' input, for their volunteering in community activities.
You are exhausted, frustrated, and pulled in too many directions.	Lack of a clear legacy and passion	Define your legacy so you can focus on your passion. Hire right, delegate effectively, and hold people accountable.

Maintenance Record

Check and date when you have started the appropriate part of the inventory, keeping in mind that none is a one-time event. All parts are subject to continuous improvement and innovation.

Date Started

___*The BOSS Parts Inventory*   _____

___*The Core*

☐ Mission defined   _____

☐ Vision defined   _____

☐ Values defined   _____

☐ Communicated   _____

___*Leadership*

☐ Competencies, characteristics defined   _____

☐ Leadership team assessment   _____

☐ Leadership development process created   _____

☐ Leadership development process
    communicated and implemented   _____

___*Customer*

☐ Customer base defined   _____

☐ Customer base communicated   _____

☐ Ongoing feedback process defined   _____

☐ Feedback Process
    communicated and implemented   _____

___*Strategic Thinking*

☐ Strategic framework developed   _____

☐ Ongoing monitoring process defined   _____

☐ Strategic framework communicated   _____

☐ Strategic thinking training implemented   _____

☐ Monitoring process and accountability
implemented   _____

___*Business Measures*

☐ Metrics defined   _____

☐ Metrics communicated   _____

☐ Ongoing monitoring process
defined and Implemented   _____

___*Processes*

☐ Processes defined and documented   _____

☐ Processes communicated   _____

☐ Continuous improvement and innovation process
created and implemented   _____

___*Employees*

☐ Interviewing process created and implemented   _____

☐ High-performance leadership system
created, communicated, and implemented   _____

___*Corporate Social Responsibility*

☐ Small–tire–track–actions determined,
communicated, and implemented   _____

☐ Large–tire–track actions determined
communicated, and implemented   _____

___BLC Culture

☐ Belonging actions identified,
communicated, and implemented   _____

☐ Learning actions identified,
communicated, and implemented   _____

☐ Contributing actions identified,
communicated, and implemented   _____

___High-Performance Results

☐ Obtained   _____

☐ Communicated   _____

Glossary

360 degree instrument/feedback: A developmental tool that provides feedback to people from their bosses, peers, and direct reports and allows comparison between those perceptions and their own self-perceptions.

Accountability: The practice of holding people answerable for their job objectives, expectations, and results.

Balanced dashboard: A group of performance measures (leading and lagging indicators) you would look at to determine how you are doing financially, the satisfaction of your customers, if your internal processes are working well, and if you are continually adding value and getting better through innovation.

Benchmarking: Researching best practices inside and outside your company and industry to determine how to improve your processes.

BLC culture: A culture of belonging, learning, and contributing in which all people are self-motivated to drive for high performance.

BOSS: The Business Operating System Solution for Enterprise Results model that is the infrastructure of a high-performance company.

Compliance: The minimum requirements to meet government standards.

Core: The mission, vision, and values of your company to which all other initiatives are connected.

Corporate social responsibility: The actions your business takes to save the earth's resources as well as contribute to the surrounding community in which it operates.

Culture: The collective beliefs, values, attitudes, and actions of the people in a company that include formal and informal norms. Culture usually is a reflection of the key leader.

Customer loyalty: The action of customers continuing to do business with you instead of your competitors; beyond customer satisfaction.

Infrastructure: The internal systems and processes in your company that support business success.

Key business process: A process (a group of related activities that produce a service or product) that people in your company must excel at to satisfy customers and other stakeholders.

Key performance areas: Areas of performance that are essential to perform the mission within the parameters of the vision.

Lagging indicators: The metrics that occur after the fact (e.g., financial measures, such as profitability).

Leadership competencies: The knowledge, skills, and abilities derived from the mission, vision, and values.

Leadership expectations: The core competencies and behaviors derived from the mission, vision, and values.

Leadership university: A process where all levels of employees and leaders are involved in continuous learning about leadership expectations (competencies and behaviors) that are derived from the core of the business (mission, vision, and values).

Leading indicators: The metrics that allow continual monitoring of goals and objectives so that modifications can be made, if necessary (e.g., employee satisfaction, process improvement).

Legacy: What people will remember about your leadership.

Metrics: Business measures of success that make up your dashboard.

Mission: The purpose of your company; the reason it exists.

Onboarding: The process of bringing new employees into your company and acquainting them with the nonadministrative aspects of the business, such as the culture, both formal and informal.

Orientation: The process of bringing new employees into your company focusing on the administrative aspects of employment, such as pay, benefits, and safety.

Reconciliation meeting: Meetings that are held between leadership and teams during a process-improvement initiative.

Restorative: Putting back more than you take; doing good, not just doing no harm.

Silos: Separate functions in a company (e.g., finance, sales, marketing) that create impermeable boundaries; also known as stovepipes.

Stakeholders: Any person or group with a vested interest in your company, such as customers, stockholders, employees.

Strategic framework: A flexible strategic plan that allows for changing conditions (opportunistic planning).

Strategic plan: A long-term plan that sets the direction, strategies, and goals for the rest of the business; the 50,000-foot view.

Strategic thinking: The thinking process that directs all people in your company to determine how their actions today will affect the business tomorrow.

Sustainability: Meeting the needs of the present without compromising the ability of future generations to meet their own needs.

Team charter: The responsibilities of a team that include the goal, the focus, the scope, deliverables, and expected results.

Values: The behaviors you expect of all people in your company; how they are expected to treat not only customers but also each other.

Vision: What your company could be at its best if everyone in the business were working on all cylinders.

Further Reading

These references are some of my favorite resources. Although some of the examples used may have become outdated, they each, at least, have a nugget of very thoughtful and useful information.

Journals and Magazines

Harvard Business Review	www.hbr.org
Leader to Leader, The Drucker Foundation	www.leadertoleader.org
Inc.	www.inc.com
Fast Company	www.fastcompany.com
CRO E-Newsletter/Corporate Social Responsibility	newsletter@thecro.com

Books

General

Edersheim, Elizabeth Hass. *The Definitive Drucker*. McGraw-Hill, 2007.

Hesselbein, Frances, Marshall Goldsmith, and Richard Beckhard. *The Organization of the Future*. Jossey-Bass, 1997.

Kotter, John and Dan Cohen. *The Heart of Change*. HBR Press 2002.

Lafley, A. G., and Ram Charan. *The Game Changer: How You Can Drive Revenue and Profit Growth with Innovation*. Crown Publishing, 2008.

Nesbitt, John. *Global Paradox*. Morrow 1994.

Reich, Robert. *The Future of Success*. Knopf 2000.

Sullivan, Gordon and Michael Harper. *Hope Is Not A Method*. Random House 1996.

Youngblood, Mark D. *Life at the Edge of Chaos*. Perceval Publishing 1997.

The Core (Mission, Vision, & Values)

Collins, Jim. *Good To Great*. Harper Business 2001.

Collins, Jim and Jerry I. Porras. *Built to Last: Successful Habits of Visionary Companies*. Harper Business 2004.

Covey, Stephen R. *The 7 Habits Of Highly Effective People*. Free Press 2004.

Quinn, Robert E. *Deep Change*. Jossey-Bass 1996.

Rao, Srikumar S. *Are You Ready To Succeed?* Hyperion 2006

Useem, Michael. *The Leadership Moment*. Times Business 1998.

Leadership

Bennis, Warren and Burt Nanus. *Leaders: The Strategies for Taking Charge*. Harper 1985.

Byham, William C., Audrey B. Smith and Matthew J. Paese. *Grow Your Own Leaders*. Prentice Hall 2002.

Clarke-Epstein, Chris. 78 Important Questions Every Leader Should Ask and Answer. AMACOM 2002.

DePree, Max. *Leadership is an Art*. Dell 1989.

Dotlich, David and Peter Cairo. *Why CEOs Fail*. John Wiley & Sons 2003.

George, Bill. *Authentic Leadership*. Jossey-Bass 2003.

Goleman, Daniel. *Emotional Intelligence*. Bantam 1994.

Hamel, Gary. *The Future of Management*. HBR Press 2007

Hesselbein, Frances, Marshall Goldsmith and Richard Beckhard. *Leader Of The Future*. Jossey-Bass 1996.

Kouzes, James M. and Barry Z. Posner. *The Leadership Challenge*. John Wiley & Sons 2008.

Kotter, John P. *John Kotter on What Leaders Really Do*. HBR Press 1999.

Kriegel, Robert J. and Louis Patler. *If it ain't broke ... Break It!* Warner Business Books 1991.

Lencioni, Patrick. *Silos, Politics and Turf Wars.* Jossey-Bass 2006.

Lombardo, Michael M. and Robert W. Eichinger. *Eighty-Eight Assignments For Development In Place.* Center for Creative Leadership 1996.

McCauley, Cynthia and, Ellen Van Velsor. *The Handbook Of Leadership Development.* Jossey-Bass 2004.

Morrell, Margot and Stephanie Capparell. *Shackleton's Way.* Vikking 2001.

Willis, Garry. *Certain Trumpets: The Nature of Leadership.* Touchstone 1995.

Leadership University

Allen, Mark. *The Corporate University Handbook.* AMACOM 2002.

Meister, Jeanne. *Corporate Universities.* McGraw-Hill 1998.

Customers

Heskitt, James L., W. Earl Sasser, Jr, and Leonard A. Schlesinger. *The Service Profit Chain.* Simon & Schuster 1997.

Ostroff, Frank. *The Horizontal Organization.* Oxford University Press 1999.

Zeithami, Valarie A. and A. Parasuraman , Leonard Barry. *Delivering Quality Service: Balance Customer Perceptions and Expectations.* Free Press 1990.

Zemke, Ron and Dick Schaaf. *The Service Edge.* NAL Books. 1989.

Strategic Thinking

Fogg, C. Davis. *Team-Based Strategic Planning: A complete Guide to Structuring, Facilitating, and Implementing the Process.* McGraw-Hill 1994.

Gibson, Rowen. *Rethinking the Future.* Nicholas Brealey Publishing 2000.

Goodstein, Leonard, Timothy Nolan, J. William Pfeiffer. *Applied Strategic Planning.* McGraw-Hill 1993.

Harmon, Fred. *Business 2010.* Kiplinger Books 2001.

Metrics

Kaplan, Robert S. and David P. Norton. *The Balanced Scorecard.* HBS Press 1996.

Process

Allan, Dave, Matt Kingdon, Kris Murrin and Daz Rudkin. *? What If! Sticky Wisdom: How To Start A Creative Revolution At Work.* Capstone 2002.

Hammer, Michael and James Champy. *Reengineering The Corporation.* HarperCollins 2001.

Sullivan, Gordon and Michael Harper. *Hope Is Not A Method.* Random House 1996.

Sutton, Robert I. *Weird Ideas That Work.* Free Press 2002.

Employees

Bennis, Warren G. and Robert J. Thomas. *Geeks & Geezers.* HBS Press 2002.

Hoevemeyer Victoria A. *High-Impact Interview Questions: 701 Behavior-Based Questions to Find the Right Person for Every Job.* AMACOM 2005.

Kaye,Beverly and Sharon Jordan-Evans. *Love 'Em or Lose 'Em: Getting Good People To Stay.* Berrett-Koehler 2005.

Katzenbach, Jon R. *Why Pride Matters More Than Money.* Crown Business 2003.

Kouzes, James M. and Barry Z. Posner. *Encouraging The Heart.* John Wiley & Sons 2003.

Littell, Robert S. *The Heart and Art of Netweaving.* Netweaving International Press 2003.

Zemke, Ron, Claire Raines and Bob Filipczak. *Generations At Work.* AMACOM 2000.

Corporate Social Responsibility

Hawken, Paul, Amory Lovins and L. Hunter Lovins. *Natural Capitalism: Creating The Next Industrial Revolution.* First Back Bay 2000

Culture

Gerstner, Jr., Louis V. *Who Says Elephants Can't Dance?* Harper Business 2003.

Schein, Edgar H. *Organizational Culture And Leadership.* John Wiley and Sons 2004.

Entrepreneurship

Gerber, Michael E. *The E-Myth Revisited.* Harper Business 1995.

About The Author

Jane Goldner, Ph.D., president and founder of The Goldner Group, is one of the nation's leading authorities on talent retention and trusted advisor to Fortune 100 Companies, government and military organizations, and small to mid-sized businesses.

For more than 25 years, Dr. Goldner's unique approach has enabled The Goldner Group to grow based on customer loyalty and referrals. The core of The Goldner Group forms the basis for her client partnerships in the areas of leadership and organizational effectiveness. Dr. Goldner leads her team by setting a goal to meet each unique client need. Building a solid leadership team and charting corporate structure for the future is critical to a company's sustainability. By engaging talent throughout the company, she identifies and implements changes to continuously improve business performance.

Dr. Goldner earned a Ph.D. in Human Resources Development from Georgia State University in Atlanta and a Masters of Arts in Counseling at the University of Alabama in Birmingham. Her undergraduate work was completed at the University of Maryland. She is also an adjunct professor at Kennesaw State University Coles College of Business

Liked the Book?
Additional Opportunities to be
Driven to Success

Formula One for High-Performance Companies: A lively and engaging keynote address

Start Your Engines for Greater Competitiveness and Profitability: A 10-point checkup workshop customized for your organization

The Scheduled Maintenance Checkup: Online parts inventory

The Business Operating System Solution for Enterprise Results Consulting: Assistance with installing any of the checkpoint processes

Contact: The Goldner Group **(404) 459-2860**

info@thegoldnergroup.com

www.thegoldnergroup.com

BUY A SHARE OF THE FUTURE IN YOUR COMMUNITY

These certificates make great holiday, graduation and birthday gifts that can be personalized with the recipient's name. The cost of one S.H.A.R.E. or one square foot is $54.17. The personalized certificate is suitable for framing and will state the number of shares purchased and the amount of each share, as well as the recipient's name. The home that you participate in "building" will last for many years and will continue to grow in value.

Here is a sample SHARE certificate:

YES, I WOULD LIKE TO HELP!

I support the work that Habitat for Humanity does and I want to be part of the excitement! As a donor, I will receive periodic updates on your construction activities but, more importantly, I know my gift will help a family in our community realize the dream of homeownership. **I would like to SHARE in your efforts against substandard housing in my community!** *(Please print below)*

PLEASE SEND ME _____ SHARES at $54.17 EACH = $ $_____

In Honor Of: _____

Occasion: (Circle One)   HOLIDAY   BIRTHDAY   ANNIVERSARY

     OTHER: _____

Address of Recipient: _____

Gift From: _____ *Donor Address:* _____

Donor Email: _____

I AM ENCLOSING A CHECK FOR $ $_____ PAYABLE TO HABITAT FOR HUMANITY OR PLEASE CHARGE MY VISA OR MASTERCARD *(CIRCLE ONE)*

Card Number _____ Expiration Date: _____

Name as it appears on Credit Card _____ Charge Amount $ _____

Signature _____

Billing Address _____

Telephone # Day _____ Eve _____

PLEASE NOTE: Your contribution is tax-deductible to the fullest extent allowed by law.
Habitat for Humanity • P.O. Box 1443 • Newport News, VA 23601 • 757-596-5553
www.HelpHabitatforHumanity.org

Printed in the USA
CPSIA information can be obtained
at www.ICGtesting.com
JSHW012035140824
68134JS00033B/3078